Into the Deep Unknown

Land of The Tent Dwellers –
A Trip Through The Wilds of Nova Scotia

Mike Parker

Pottersfield Press, Lawrencetown Beach, Nova Scotia, Canada

Copyright © Mike Parker 2013

All rights reserved. No part of this publication may be reproduced or used or stored in any form or by any means – graphic, electronic or mechanical, including photocopying – or by any information storage or retrieval system without the prior written permission of the publisher. Any requests for photocopying, recording, taping or information storage and retrieval systems shall be directed in writing to the publisher or to Access Copyright, The Canadian Copyright Licensing Agency, 1 Yonge Street, Suite 800, Toronto, Ontario, Canada M5E 1E5 (www.AccessCopyright.ca). This also applies to classroom use.

Library and Archives Canada Cataloguing in Publication

Parker, Mike, 1952-
Into the deep unknown : land of the tent dwellers--a trip through the wilds of Nova Scotia / Mike Parker.
Includes excerpts from Dr. M.B. Miller's 1910 fishing trip through the Keji and the Toby with hunting and fishing guides.
Includes bibliographical references.
ISBN 978-1-897426-46-3

1. Canoes and canoeing--Nova Scotia--History. 2. Canoe camping--Nova Scotia--History.
3. Fishing guides--Nova Scotia--History. 4. Hunting guides--Nova Scotia--History.
5. Outdoor life--Nova Scotia--History--Pictorial works. 6. Nova Scotia--Description and travel--History--Anecdotes.
I. Title.
GV776.N6P37 2013   917.16'2043   C2013-901312-1

Cover design by Gail LeBlanc

Cover photo: Nova Scotia Archives

We acknowledge the financial support of the Government of Canada through the Canada Book Fund for our publishing activities. We acknowledge the support of the Canada Council for the Arts, which last year invested $157 million to bring the arts to Canadians throughout the country. Nous remercions le Conseil des arts du Canada de son soutien. L'an dernier, le Conseil a investi 157 millions de dollars pour mettre de l'art dans la vie des Canadiennes et des Canadiens de tout le pays. We also thank the Province of Nova Scotia for its support through the Department of Communities, Culture and Heritage.

Pottersfield Press
83 Leslie Road
East Lawrencetown, Nova Scotia, Canada, B2Z 1P8
Website: www.PottersfieldPress.com
To order, phone 1-800-NIMBUS9 (1-800-646-2879) www.nimbus.ns.ca

Publisher's Note

Into the Deep Unknown leads us into the unique landscape of southwest Nova Scotia, immortalized by Albert Bigelow Paine in his 1908 classic *The Tent Dwellers*. Now known as the Tobeatic Wilderness Area and Kejimkujik National Park, it is internationally recognized by UNESCO as the Southwest Nova Biosphere Reserve, an area of natural and cultural heritage.

In his fifteenth book, Mike Parker takes us on a 1910 canoe trip through the words of Dr. M.B. Miller, an American who in 1911 published a first-hand, six-part account of his voyage through Keji and the Toby with legendary Nova Scotia guides. Mike adds great depth and breadth to Miller's account by including 422 vintage photos of the backcountry and the legendary hunting and fishing guides of the area with detailed supportive text.

Into the Deep Unknown adds to and continues the story of the woods and waters of Nova Scotia and the people who drew their livelihoods from them that Mike began in his first books *Guides of the North Woods*, *Wood Chips & Beans*, and *Where Moose and Trout Abound*.

Tent Dwellers 1992 – daughter Emily, three, and son Matthew, five, Sixth Lake. This book is for you.

Tent Dwellers 2012 – Emily and Matt pose with "Jacques Coulac, the Lumberjack," Sixth Lake.
Big enough now to carry the gear for Dad.

Contents

Acknowledgements	9
Sources	10
Photo Credits	11
Map: Southwest Nova Scotia Canoe Routes c.1910	14-15
Introduction	17
Chapter 1: In the Wake of The Tent Dwellers	63
Photo Album I: The Tent Dwellers	91
Chapter 2: Long Pull to the Shelburne	135
Chapter 3: A Stern Unfruitful Land	163
Photo Album II: Gateway to the Interior	191
Chapter 4: A Dash of Peril Now and Then	211
Chapter 5: Yearning for Civilization	237
Phtoto Album III: He-Woodsmen of the North	247
Conclusion	273

Acknowledgements

This book would not have been possible without the assistance, expertise and generosity of many. Thanks and appreciation goes out to Lesley Choyce, Peggy Amirault, Julia Swan and Gail LeBlanc of Pottersfield Press; Kim Walker, Shelburne County Archives; Peter Crowell, Argyle Township Court House Archives; Sheryl Stanton, Admiral Digby Museum; Dawn Nickerson, Barrington Museum; Gerry Parker; Alain Belliveau; Bob Johnston; Chris Johnston; Colin Gray; Bob Guscott; Neil Brennan; Lillian Perry; Phil Scott; Sandra Phinney; Mary Harris; Gary Castle; Philip Hoad; Philip Moscovitch; Linda Miller; Maxine Townsend; Bud Inglis; Dave Freeman; Brian Braganza; Peter McInroy; Jonathan Sheppard; Bob Thexton; Milford House; Lois Yorke, Philip Hartling and all the staff at Nova Scotia Archives and Records Management. A special debt of gratitude goes to Tim Coggeshall and Archer Turnbull, whose family albums provided a treasure trove of images. Also Dr. Jim Morrison and the Helen Creighton Folklore Society for financial assistance in the form of a grant-in-aid. A hearty thanks to Helen, Emily and Matt. My sincere apologies to anyone who may have contributed but find themselves omitted. No slight was intended.

The following sources were consulted in the creation of this book:

Breck, Edward. *The Way of the Woods.* New York: G.P. Putnam, 1908.

Breck, Edward. *Wilderness Pets at Camp Buckshaw.* New York: Broughton, Mifflin Company, 1910.

Green, Norm; Moreira William; Sheppard, Tom. *Keji.* Halifax, Nova Scotia: Nimbus Publishing Ltd., 2005.

Inglis, Bud. *Backwoods Cabins of Nova Scotia.* Hantsport, Nova Scotia: Lancelot Press, 1990.

Inglis, Bud. *Through Deepest Nova Scotia.* Halifax, Nova Scotia: Nimbus Publishing Ltd., 1999.

Leefe, John; Morrison, Jim; Evans, Millie; Mullen, Eric. *Kejimkujik National Park.* Four East Publications, 1981.

Milford and Area History Group. *Through the Woods.* Self-Published, 2005.

Morrison, Jim; Friend, Lawrence. *We Have Held Our Own, The Western Interior of Nova Scotia, 1800-1940.* Parks Canada, 1981.

Paine, Albert Bigelow. *The Tent Dwellers.* New York: The Outing Publishing Co., 1908.

Parker, Mike. *Guides of the North Woods.* Halifax, Nova Scotia: Nimbus Publishing Ltd., 1990.

Parker, Mike. *Wood Chips & Beans.* Halifax, Nova Scotia: Nimbus Publishing Ltd., 1992.

Parker, Mike. *Where Moose and Trout Abound.* Halifax, Nova Scotia: Nimbus Publishing Ltd., 1995.

Parker, Mike. *Rivers of Yesterday.* Halifax, Nova Scotia: Nimbus Publishing Ltd., 1997.

Ricker, Darlene. *L'sitkuk, The Story of the Bear River Mi'kmaw Community.* Lockeport, Nova Scotia: Roseway Publishing, 1997.

Smith, Andrew. *Paddling the Tobeatic.* Halifax, Nova Scotia: Nimbus Publishing Ltd., 2004.

Whitehead, Ruth Holmes. *Tracking Doctor Lonecloud.* Fredericton, New Brunswick: Goose Lane Editions and Nova Scotia Museum, 2002.

Photo Credits

LEGEND

ADM: Admiral Digby Museum
AHS: Annapolis Heritage Society
ATCHA: Argyle Township Court House Archives
B: Bottom
BM: Barrington Museum
L: Left
MHS: Milford Historical Society
NSA: Nova Scotia Archives
PC: Personal Collection
R: Right
SCM: Shelburne County Museum
T: Top

MAP PP. 14-15 BOB GUSCOTT

MAP P. 16 ALAIN BELLIVEAU

INTRODUCTION

p.17 Tim Coggeshall
pp.18-19 PC
pp. 20-21 Ralph Harris
pp.22-23 PC
pp.24-25 NSA
p.26 (L) Colin Gray (R) BM
p.27 (T) NSA, (B) PC
pp.28-30 NSA
pp.32-33 NSA

pp.35-38 NSA
p.40 NSA
p.41 (L) NSA (R) PC
pp.42-44 NSA
p.45 Tim Coggeshall
p.46 Robin Wyllie
pp.47-50 NSA
p.51 (LT, B) NSA (R) PC
pp.52-53 ADM
p.54 (T) NSA (B) Bob Johnston
p.55 PC
p.56 SCM
p.57 (TL, BL) NSA (TR) Scott Family (BR) PC
p.58 NSA
pp.59-61 PC
p.62 NSA

CHAPTER 1

pp.64-65 (T) Tim Coggeshall (B) MHS
p.66 Tim Coggeshall
p.67 MHS
p.68 NSA
p.69 PC
p.70 NSA
pp.71-72 PC
pp.73-75 Tim Coggeshall
pp.76-77 (T) MHS (B) NSA
pp.78-80 NSA

p.81 Bob Johnston
p.82 MHS
p.83 Tim Coggeshall
p.84 MHS
pp.85-86 Tim Coggeshall
p.87 MHS
p.88 Tim Coggeshall
p.89 Scott Family
p.90 Tim Coggeshall

PHOTO ALBUM I

p.91 Ralph Harris
p.92 (T) PC (B) NSA
pp.93-112 Tim Coggeshall
p.113 (T, BL) Tim Coggeshall (BR) NSA
pp.114-124 Tim Coggeshall
p.125 PC
pp.126-134 Tim Coggeshall

CHAPTER 2

p.136 (T) MHS (B) Archer Turnbull
p.137 Tim Coggeshall
pp 138-142 NSA
p.144 Tim Coggeshall
p.145 PC
p.146 ATCHA
p.147 Archer Turnbull
p.148 Tim Coggeshall
p.149 NSA
p.151(T) Archer Turnbull (B) NSA
pp.152-153 NSA
p.154 Dave Freeman
p.155 Tim Coggeshall
p.156 Dave Freeman
p.157 PC
pp158-159 NSA
p.160 AHS
p.161 Tim Coggeshall
p.162 (L) Tim Coggeshall (R) Archer Turnbull

CHAPTER 3

p.164 PC
p.165 NSA
p166 Tim Coggeshall
p.167 Philip Hoad
p.168 (T) Colin Gray (B) Philip Moscovitch
p.169 Archer Turnbull
pp.170-171 NSA
p.172 MHS
p.173 Colin Gray
p.174 Chris Johnston
p.175 ATCHA
pp.176-177 Colin Gray
p.178 (L) MHS (R) Colin Gray
pp.179-180 Archer Turnbull
p.181 MHS
p.182 PC
p.183 Colin Gray
pp.184 NSA
p.186 Ralph Harris
p.187 MHS
p.188 Tim Coggeshall

PHOTO ALBUM II

p.191 Archer Turnbull
p.192 PC
p.193 (TL) NSA (TR,B) PC
pp.194-198 NSA
p.199 Sheryl Stanton, ADM
pp.200-202 Archer Turnbull
p.203 (T) Vincent Rice (B) PC
p.204 PC
pp.205-207 Archer Turnbull
p.208 (T) PC (B) Archer Turnbull
p.209 Archer Turnbull
p.210 (T) NSA (B) Archer Turnbull

CHAPTER 4

p.212 Tim Coggeshall
p.213 Archer Turnbull
p.215 Tim Coggeshall
p.216 Colin Gray
p.217 MHS
pp.218-220 ATCHA
p.221 Scott family
p.222-223 ATCHA
p.224 NSA
p.225 ATCHA
p.226 NSA
p227 ATCHA
p.229 PC
p.230 NSA
p.231 Scott Family
p.232 MHS
p.233 PC
p.234 Ralph Harris
p.235 (T) ADM (B) NSA
p.236 Ralph Harris

CHAPTER 5

pp.238-239 ATCHA
pp.241-243 NSA
p.244 MHS
p.245 (T) PC (B) Dave Freeman
p.246 (T) PC (B) Robin Wylie

PHOTO ALBUM III

p.247 Linda Miller
pp.248-249 NSA
pp.250-251 Tim Coggeshall
p.252 NSA
pp.253-254 PC
p.255 (T) Lindsey Peck (B) Tim Coggeshall
p.256 (TL) NSA (TR,B) PC
p.257 (TL) NSA (TR) SCM
pp.258-260 PC
p.261 (T) PC (B) Lindsey Peck
p.262 PC
p.263 (T) PC (B) Lindsey Peck
p.264 (T) PC (B) SCM
p.265 PC
p.266 (T) Lindsey Peck, (B) PC
pp.267-269 PC
p.270 NSA
p.271 Scott Family
p.272 (T) Scott Family (B) PC

CONCLUSION

p.274 PC
p.275 (T) Linda Miller (B) PC
p.276 PC
p.277 (T) PC (B) Sandra Phinney
p.278 PC
p.279 Philip Moscovitch
p.280 Sandra Phinney

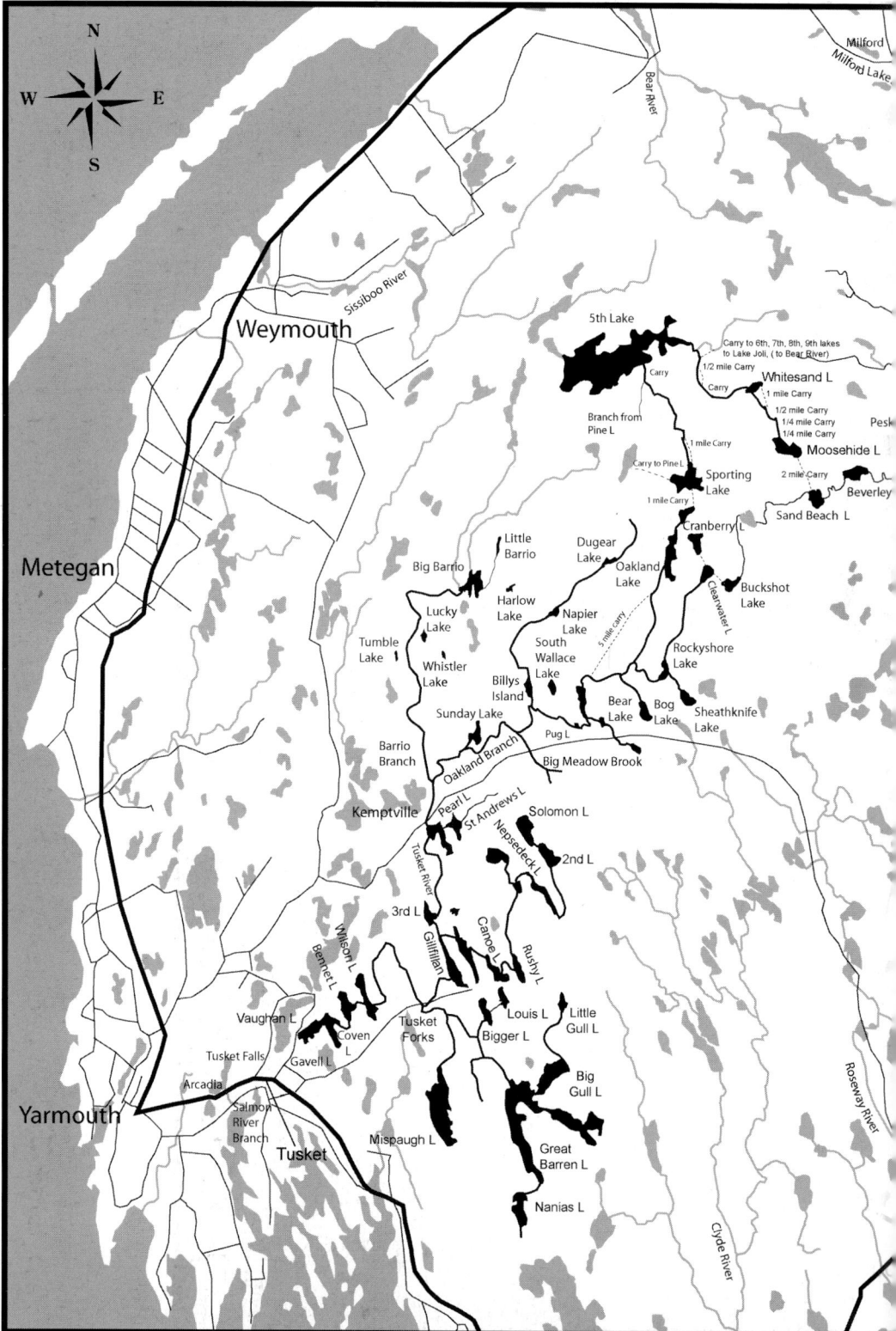

This overlay map was produced from a rough sketch which accompanied Dr. M.B. Miller's six-part *Forest & Stream* series in 1911 retracing a 1910 canoe trip through southwest Nova Scotia.

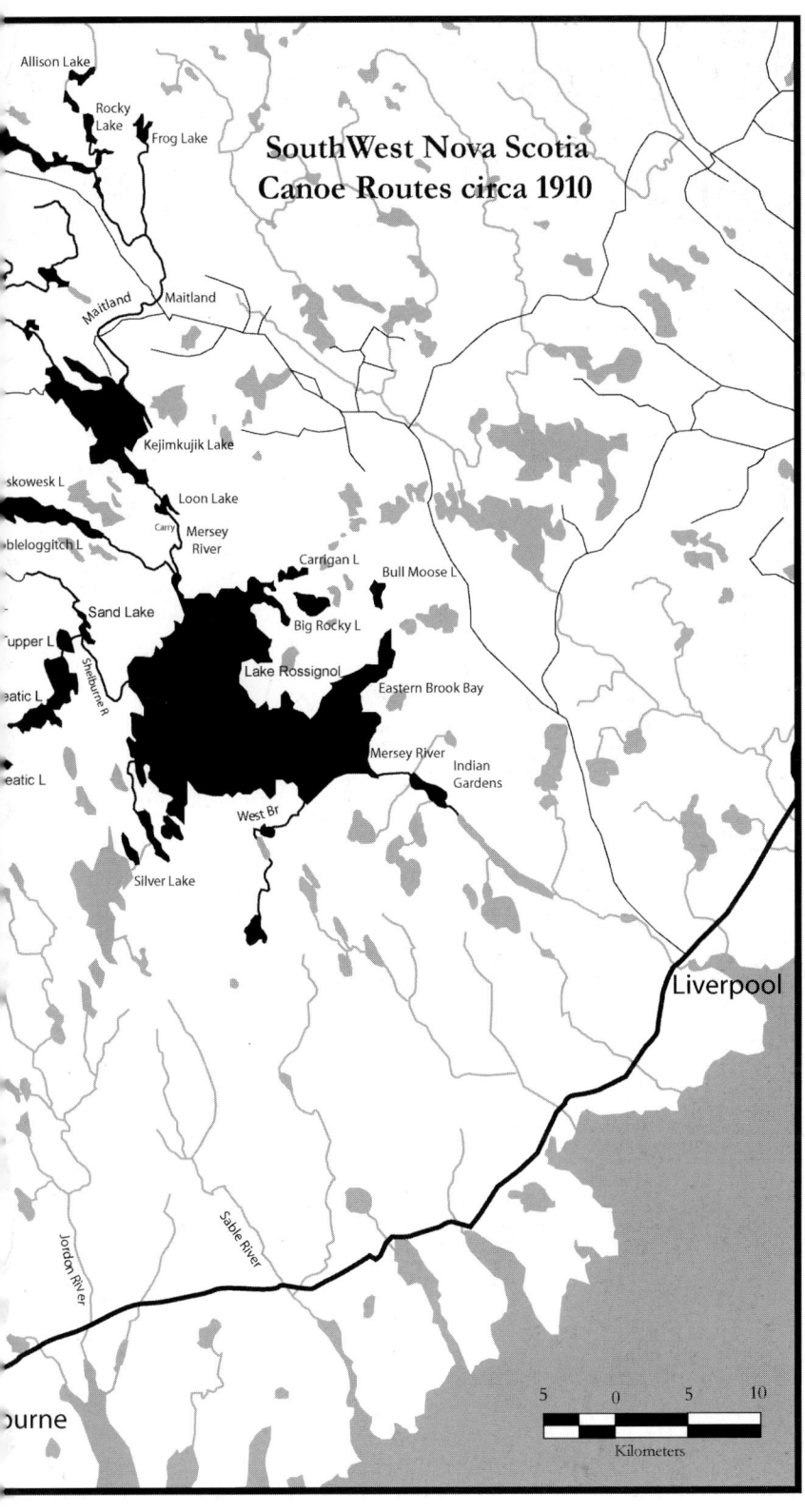

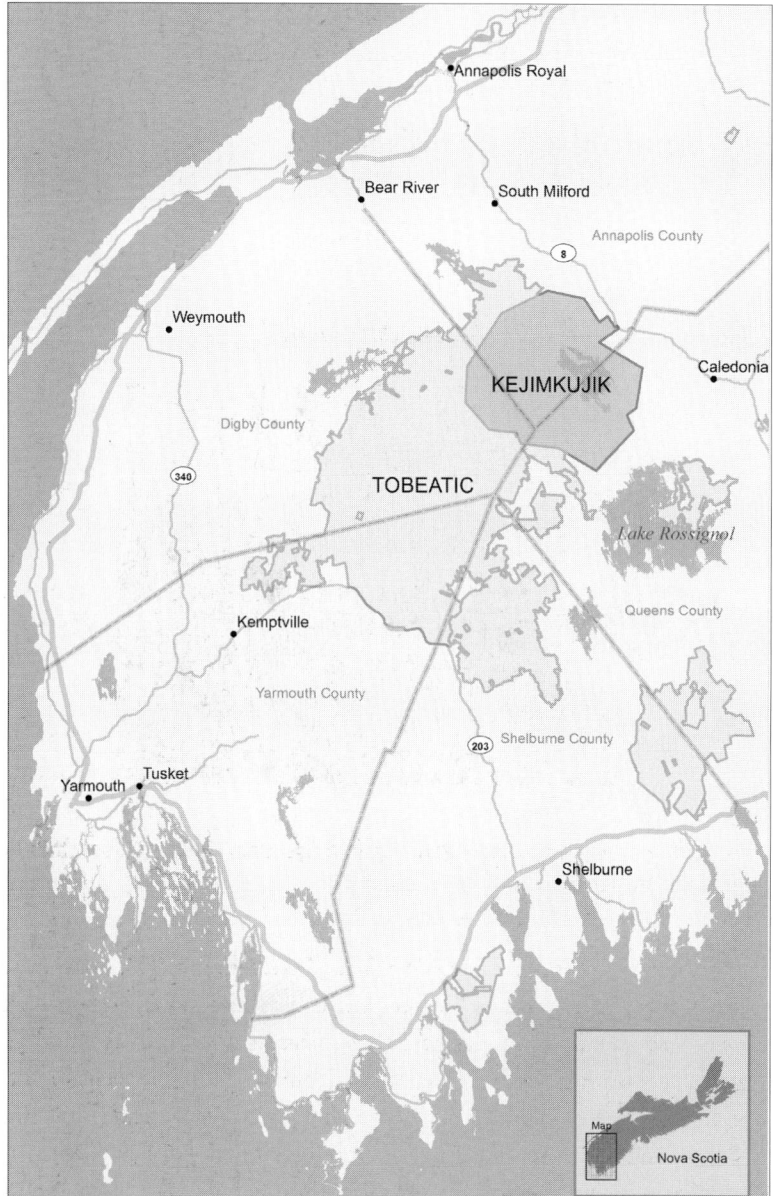

The Land of the Tent Dwellers is a canoe-tripper's paradise, encompassing the five southwestern counties of Nova Scotia – Annapolis, Digby, Yarmouth, Shelburne and Queens. At its core is the Tobeatic Wilderness Area and Kejimkujik National Park and Historic Site of Canada that protect nearly 875 square miles (142,000 hectares) of diversified forest and wetlands. Contained within are hundreds of lakes interconnected like the spokes of a wheel by hundreds more rivers, streams and ancient portages which "could take a lifetime" to explore.

On average, no point in Nova Scotia is more than 40 miles from the sea, but here the distance could be 400 for the sense of isolation and tranquility that pervades the region. These five counties are the Southwest Nova Biosphere Reserve, a "UNESCO designated and internationally recognized region of natural and cultural heritage," currently one of only two biosphere reserves in Nova Scotia, 16 in all of Canada and 610 worldwide in 117 countries.

Introduction

Unspoiled woods and waters, abundant game and legendary guides were the cornerstones on which tourism was built in Nova Scotia.

When Albert Bigelow Paine penned *The Tent Dwellers* in 1908, tourism as we know it was non-existent. Nova Scotia's "sea-bound coast" had yet to be immortalized in song. Its lighthouses were saving lives in danger; they were not endangered and in need of saving. Lunenburg was a working-class fishing port, not a world-class heritage site. Whales were hunted, not watched. The last of the tall ships were plying their trade, not lining up for parades of sail. Nova Scotia license plates were nondescript, not scripted with *Canada's Ocean Playground*. Rural communities were vibrant and populated places, not stagnant and abandoned. Cities were places to escape, not embrace. You paddled canoes made of wood and birchbark, not fibreglass and plastic; slept in the out-of-doors on boughs and under canvas, not foam and nylon; navigated the woods and waters using nature's "signposts" and a compass, not a satellite and GPS; kept warm and dry wearing wool and oilskins, not Gore-Tex and Thinsulate; canned beans and marmalade trumped freeze dried and trail mix.

Albert Bigelow Paine (1861-1937) was born in New Bedford, Massachusetts. He began his working career in the American Midwest as a photographer and dealer of photographic supplies but changed vocations in 1895 to become a full-time writer. Spending most of his life in Europe, Paine was a highly successful author of fiction, humour and verse, editor of several magazines and a long-serving member of the Pulitzer Prize committee. His claim to fame was a three-volume biography of Samuel Langhorne Clemens, a.k.a. Mark Twain (1835-1910), whom he lived and travelled with for four years.

Albert Bigelow Paine (left), shown here playing billiards with Mark Twain, bookended *The Tent Dwellers* between *The Van Dwellers* (1901) and *The Ship Dwellers* (1910).

Paine could never have envisioned the impact *The Tent Dwellers* would have on Nova Scotia tourism, nor the cult-like following the book would attract from the outset that continues today among outdoor enthusiasts. *The Tent Dwellers* is a lighthearted account describing "a classic camping and fishing adventure in the unchartered wilderness" of southwestern Nova Scotia that Paine took c.1903 with fellow American Eddie Breck, who organized the trip, accompanied by two Nova Scotia guides, Del (the Stout) Thomas and Charles (the Strong) Charleton. Amongst all the mishaps and missteps chronicled by Paine the tyro woodsman is Thoreau-like prose from Paine the philosopher that rings as true today as when put to paper more than a hundred years ago.

"The north wood does not offer welcome or respond readily to the lover of conventional luxury and the smaller comforts of living. Luxury is there, surely, but it is the luxury that rewards effort, and privation, and toil. It is the comfort of food and warmth and dry clothes after a day of endurance – a day of wet, and dragging weariness, and bitter chill. ... It is the preciousness of isolation, the remoteness from men who dig up and tear down and destroy, who set whistles to tooting and bells to jingling – who shriek themselves hoarse in the market place and make the world ugly and discordant, and life a short and fevered span in which the soul has a chance to become no more than a feeble and crumpled thing. ... The wilderness will welcome you, and teach you and take you to its heart. And you will find your own soul there; and the discovery will be worth while!"

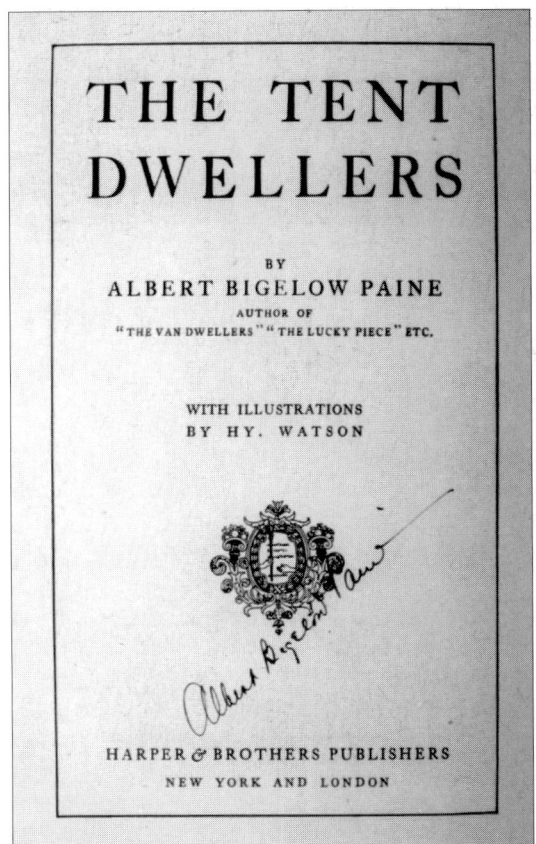 

On the left is the title page from an autographed 1908 first edition of *The Tent Dwellers*. Reprinted on at least three occasions in the United States and Canada, the book came to prominence locally with a "Nova Scotia edition" in 1982, followed by a commemorative 100th anniversary release in 2008 shown at right. American illustrator Henry Sumner "Hy" Watson (1868-1933), whose drawings often graced the covers of *Field & Stream* and *Outdoor Life*, produced the original artwork for the book. Watson may have based his sketches on photographs taken by Paine during the canoe trip, but a search for the elusive treasure trove has yielded nothing.

At one particularly nostalgic point in the book Paine waxed eloquently, "I was filled with the feeling that must have come over those old Canadian voyageurs who were first to make their way through the northlands, threading the network of unknown waters. I could not get rid of the idea that we were pioneers in this desolate spot, and so far as sportsmen were concerned, it might be that we were."

Such prose stirred the imagination then, and still does. But Paine and his entourage were not the first or even close to being the first. Others had canoed through the same country in the mid to late 1800s. Thanks to Paine, however, many would follow in the wake of *The Tent Dwellers*, a few of whom left their own accounts, one of which forms the backdrop for *Into The Deep Unknown*.

Billy Meuse, a Mi'kmaq guide from Bear River, holds up two speckled trophies somewhere on the Sissiboo waters in Digby County, part of the canoe route taken by three American "sports" – Dr. M.B. Miller and two friends – in 1910.

In 1911, an American sportsman known only as Dr. M.B. Miller wrote a lengthy, informative and highly entertaining story that was published as a six-part weekly series (September 2 to October 7) in *Forest & Stream* magazine. In "From Rossignol to Tusket," Miller recounted a canoe trip he and two physician friends took in 1910 through the wilds of southwestern Nova Scotia. Many components from *The Tent Dwellers* are present in Miller's writing – Paine, Breck, Del the Stout and Charles the Strong, Milford House, moose, porcupines, legions of trout "as big as your leg," and an underlying sense of concern for conservation.

They paddled familiar waters at the outset – the Mersey, Kejimkujik, Rossignol, the Shelburne, Peskawa, and Pebbleoggitch – but then Miller and company struck "into the unknown" to search for routes off the beaten track. While Miller proved himself equally adept at turning a line as Paine, the medical practitioner distinguished himself from the humorist in that he wasn't a newcomer to our backwoods, having "visited Nova Scotia for several years" on fishing trips.

Unfortunately, little to nothing is known about any of the three doctors other than what Miller chose to share briefly in the first installment of his *Forest & Stream* article (which comprises Chapter 1 of *Into The Deep Unknown*). From an obituary of one member of the group, Dr. J. Gurney Taylor (1872-1956), we learn Taylor was highly respected in pediatrics and internal medicine, was "a gregarious individual … [with] a wide circle of friends … outgoing, easy of contact and urbane in his personal relations." Dr. Taylor was the trip's designated photographer; eighteen of his pictures illustrated the *Forest & Stream* series, some showing the central characters at work and rest, but sadly, like Paine's purported collection, the years have erased any trails leading to their whereabouts.

Bear River merchant and professional photographer Ralph Harris, right, with Mi'kmaq guide Billy Meuse. Harris produced hundreds of negatives and prints during the Elite Sports Tourist Era featuring hunting, fishing and camping scenes. Most of his collection was destroyed in a 1970 fire.

Into The Deep Unknown is an extensively illustrated sporting journal, combining the doctors' 1910 "pilgrimage" through the backcountry of southwestern Nova Scotia with 422 vintage photographs and supportive text. Many images have been selected and placed to enhance the storyline, others because they are historically significant in their own right, and a few for pure interest's sake. Nearly 200 are compiled into three "photo albums" inserted at relevant points in the book. *Into the Deep Unknown* focuses upon the middle years of the Elite Sport Tourist Era, a period that could just as easily be called The Tent Dwellers Era. For a better overall understanding of the book and the evolution of guiding in Nova Scotia, the introduction will provide a brief overview of the three tourist eras, beginning with the military tourists garrisoned at Halifax in the mid-1800s.

In an article entitled "American Tourism in Nova Scotia, 1871-1940," Dr. James H. Morrison breaks down early tourism into three distinct eras. "The first, that of the military tourist, began in the early nineteenth century and lasted until 1871, drawing its clientele almost exclusively from the officer class stationed in the various provincial urban centres. ... The second stage covered a period of some seventy years from 1871 to 1940, and can generally be considered to be the 'elite sport tourist' period; unlike the first stage, which consisted for the most part of British 'tourists,' this second period included mostly Americans. ... The third and final period [the Mobile Tourist Era] has been one of drastic change. Since 1940 there has been a tourist explosion, due for the most part to economic boom times and the widespread use of the automobile. ... The clientele ... changed from a majority of Americans in the second period to a mix of Americans and Canadians [in the third]."

Captain William Chearnley, "a hot-headed but warm-hearted Irishman, the king of local sportsmen ... is indelibly associated with the history of sport in [Nova Scotia]."

Two British officers, William Chearnley and Campbell Hardy, stood head and shoulders above all others during the Military Tourist Era. From the November 5, 1921, issue of *The Acadian Recorder* we learn that "William and John Chearnley were brothers [who] came to Nova Scotia in the early [1830s] ... William was a Captain in the 8th King's Regiment and remained in Halifax after the regiment left, later becoming a Captain in the Chebucto Grays, a unit which was later merged into the 63rd Reg. of Militia. He was made a Lieut.-Colonel of the Halifax Volunteer Battalion in 1865 and died in Boston on July 9th 1871. His brother John died at Halifax on March 28, 1867. Both brothers were great hunters and came to Newfoundland every year for Caribou. ..."

British officers hunted and fished throughout Nova Scotia and New Brunswick in the mid-1800s, some even venturing to Newfoundland. This carved record of the Chearnley brothers' 1853 visit to Newfoundland was photographed in 1920.

Both William and John were Freemasons, members of the Virgin Lodge in Halifax. They left evidence of their 1853 hunting trip to Newfoundland, as shown by this photo taken in 1920. *The Acadian Recorder* described the scene: "Near the foot of Mount Sykes, 1,913 feet high, and amid virgin forest stands a gigantic birch tree, a monarch of its kind, its exact location being where the Birchy Stream begins its course into Sandy Lake. This spot has been known for years as Freemason's Point. This king of trees is some thirty feet in circumference and was discovered by some Nova Scotia Freemasons over sixty years ago [1850s] when travel in Newfoundland was not as comfortable as it is today. Desiring to perpetuate their visit, these pioneers scaled off the bark until the bole was exposed. On this they carved a number of symbols of Masonry with their names. Of the latter those most clear are William and John Chearnley of Halifax and James Cope, the date being September 17, 1853. ... James Cope was an Indian guide who lived at Shubenacadie, Nova Scotia, and often went with the Chearnleys to Newfoundland on their hunting expeditions. He had but one arm, but was wonderfully skilful in shooting and woodcraft. He will best be remembered as the Indian who discovered the Rawdon gold mines [Hants County, Nova Scotia]."

Royal Artillery Park Officers' Mess, Halifax, 1890s. The moose head and antlers may be trophies from the Chearnley era.

William Chearnley, who served as Indian Agent after retiring from the military, kept an unpublished journal of his sporting trips and related musings. He drew upon the following undated journal entry on at least one occasion, possibly to regale fellow sportsmen during an after dinner talk at the Royal Artillery Park Officers' Mess.

"Anecdotes concerning some famous Indian hunters, great rogues, I admit, but still friends of mine simply for the reason that I am well aware they were fond of me, and in their lifetime shewed [sic] me many a day and nights – grand sports. ...

"I will pull up this one about Joe Philips. There are very few Indians about Lunenburgh [sic] County. Three families I know of, but those for the most part keep on the seaboard, and seldom visit the interior. Joe Philips was its only moose and bear hunter for years. He always found a ready market for his meat in Lunenburgh town, almost invariably taking it to sell there. ...

"He was bound into that place one evening minus wild meat. A large Common Land has to be crossed before entering streets of this town settlement. On that lay a dead horse. J.P. waited for the shades of evening, skinned a hind quarter of that animal, and bright and early in the morning, he fastened on his back Indian fashion, and trotted to town with it. On his arrival he was welcomed and very quickly sold off his moose meat to his excellent friends. Twelve o'clock found him on the Common again but it was to cross it in a hurry, then for the forest. He never ventured amongst the Dutch folk again. He heard afterwards that he had been found out. I taxed him with it when he once made a visit to my camp at night. He was away in the morning early, and I never saw him again."

Fishing the Musquodoboit River near Halifax, 1890s. The sawmill dam, upper left, blocked spawning salmon from migrating upriver. In the early 1850s, the removal of dams, nets and sawdust siltation from rivers to protect fish habitat was a priority for the Game and Inland Fishery Protection Society of Nova Scotia, the first of its kind in Canada and second in North America.

In an 1839 journal entry that gives anglers reason to salivate with envy, Chearnley wrote, "I caught 48 salmon in the Musquodoboit. Had ten days leave from my Regiment. I took one day journey there and another to return, Sunday of course was not a fishing day; consequently I had only seven clear days fishing. ... I lost at least 30 of a good size, all captured were full sized. One fish ... proved to be 33 lbs. weight. The second morning being alone I captured 6 salmon before breakfast time 8 o'clock. Several trout were taken, one *Salmo Ferox* weighing 63 lbs. at the Falls above Crawford's Falls; lost its mate, the male fish, after a great fight."

William Chearnley built 16 crude hunting and fishing camps during the 1850s in Halifax, Guysborough and Colchester counties. He notes in his journal that nearly all were "maliciously" destroyed by local settlers. Could such acts of vandalism have been in response to the efforts of British officers, such as Chearnley, to establish Nova Scotia's first game laws and conservation measures? The average settler saw this as nothing more than an attempt by the privileged few to control the game for their exclusive use and enjoyment; local residents depended upon moose, caribou and salmon for daily table fare as well as income garnered from selling wild meat to markets in Halifax and Saint John.

Left: Yarmouth County guide Ellison Gray tries to lure an unsuspecting bull moose with a birchbark calling horn. Right: Hamming it up for the camera near Barrington, Shelburne County, early 1900s.

Caribou and moose were hunted and snared unmercifully in the early to mid-1800s, causing sportsmen like William Chearnley and Campbell Hardy to call for measures to stop the carnage. But as one British officer noted, "The [Game and Inland Fishery Protection] Society then was neither rich nor powerful enough to cope with all the ... abuses, although the members gave both time and money to endeavor to have the laws carried out." Forest fires, roads, settlements, railways and lumbering all contributed to the eventual loss of caribou and moose habitat which resulted in their demise and decline.

Moose hunting season was permanently closed province-wide in 1937, a restriction still in effect today on mainland Nova Scotia where the approximately 1,000 animals that remain are protected under endangered species status. A controlled hunt (10,000 applicants for 345 licenses in 2012) is currently permitted on Cape Breton Island, which is home to an estimated 2,500 to 3,500 moose, a sub-species (*Alces andersonii*) introduced in 1947 from Alberta to replace Nova Scotia's native moose (*Alces americana*).

One of the last legally killed caribou in Nova Scotia, taken on the Southwest Barren, northern Victoria County, September 23, 1912. Caribou were effectively extinct throughout mainland Nova Scotia in 1905 and on Cape Breton Island by 1912, although occasional sightings continued for a few years.

White-tail deer were reintroduced to Nova Scotia in the 1890s. There is archaeological evidence they were here before Europeans arrived but had died off. By the early 1900s they had multiplied to the point of becoming the province's principal big game animal, a status they retain today.

Major General Campbell Hardy R.A., sportsman, naturalist, artist and author; 1831-1919.

    The second sportsman extraordinaire, and unquestionably the most widely acclaimed from the Military Tourist Era, was Campbell Hardy, whose obituary (partially reprinted here) was written by Harry Piers (1870-1940), an esteemed historian and long-serving curator of the Nova Scotia Museum in Halifax. Piers believed "… the passing of General Hardy … calls for special notice, as he was a notable man who had taken the deepest interest in this province and who did much through his writings to draw the attention of sportsmen and naturalists to this field."

Portrait of Campbell Hardy, sketched by an anonymous British officer.

Piers wrote: "Campbell Hardy was born at Norwich, Norfolk, England, on 10th October 1831, and was the eldest son of the Rev. Charles Hardy, M.A., of Whitewell, Hertfordshire. In the earliest years of the nineteenth century [Rev. Hardy] had been a chaplain on one of King George's frigates on the North American Station, and had visited Nova Scotia. ... Young Hardy was educated for the military profession at the Royal Military Academy, Woolwich. He entered the Royal Artillery as an ensign on 19th Dec., 1849, and became lieutenant on 11th Aug., 1851.

"To live and camp in the great backwoods of Canada had been his ambition in early youth, and in Feb. 1852, at the age of twenty, he came to Halifax and remained here till August 1867, a period of fifteen and a half years. ... Like very many other military men of the period, he was a most enthusiastic sportsman, and being keenly interested in all he met with in forest and field, he became a good naturalist, and his skilful pencil enabled him to delineate with much truth the scenes and objects about him. In Andrew Downs [who opened North America's first professional zoo at Halifax in 1847] he found a field naturalist who could assist him with knowledge of the animal life. He immediately began to take advantage of the sport which the New World offered in abundance, and was particularly attracted by the king of our game, the moose.

Hardy's sketch of salmon fishing at Pabineau Falls on the Nepisiquit River, New Brunswick, 1852.

A Campbell Hardy print of a fishing camp on the Musquodoboit River, Halifax County, 1853.

"He was present at the inauguration of the Provincial Association for the Protection of the Inland Fisheries and Game of the Province of Nova Scotia, under the presidency of Capt. [William] Chearnley, at Halifax, in March 1853, and was one of the original members.

"The following mention of some of his principal sporting trips during his first three years' sojourn here, will give an idea of his activity ... In July 1852 he made a twelve-days' salmon fishing trip on the Nepisiquit River, New Brunswick [for an account see *Rivers of Yesterday: A New Brunswick Hunting and Fishing Journal*]. In the winter of 1852-3, he was on an unsuccessful moose-hunt with the veteran guide, Joe Cope, in the neighbourhood of Petite (Walton, Nova Scotia). On 26-28 Feb. 1853, he and a companion again went moose-hunting with that most noted of Indian guides, John Williams, and Francis Paul and his son Joe, at Ship Harbour Big Lake, Halifax County, but saw no moose. They then moved camp and were from 1st to 3rd March at Fish Lake (now Scraggy Lake) in the Ship Harbour backwoods, and there on 4th March he got his first moose, a fine bull, nearly 7 feet to the shoulder and weighing 1,100 or 1,200 lbs., and the whole party brought down six moose in one day [see *Where Moose and Trout Abound*].

"In May, 1852 or '53, he was trout-fishing at Frederick's Lake, St. Margaret's Bay Road, with eccentric Charles Frederick; and June found him fishing sea-trout at the head of Musquodoboit Harbour, Halifax County. From 19th Aug. to 10th Sept., 1853, he was on a canoe voyage in New Brunswick from Bathurst up the Restigouche River, fishing salmon, and down the St. John River to Fredericton [see *Rivers of Yesterday: A New Brunswick Hunting and Fishing Journal*]. In Sept. of the same year on his return from New Brunswick, he was moose-calling with Indians Christopher Paul and Tom Philips at Long Lake, Ponhook Lakes, Halifax and Hants Counties, and in October 1854 he and a friend were again moose-hunting at Fish Lake (Scraggy Lake), with guide Joe Paul and another Indian [for the latter account, see *Where Moose and Trout Abound*]. These trips he fully described in his first book.

"As a result of these various shooting and fishing expeditions, and with the knowledge he had gained of our forests, trees, plants, mammals, fish, and of the Micmac and Malecite Indians and their legends, he wrote his first work, *Sporting Adventures in the New World; or Days and Nights of Moose-Hunting in the Pine Forests of Acadia*, published in two volumes of about three hundred pages each, in London in 1855, with two coloured illustrations from his own sketches [see pages 32 and 33]. Particulars are given of the flies and fishing tackle required, and of the methods pursued in moose-hunting, etc., and the work concludes with a catalogue of the birds of Nova Scotia, with scientific names, 121 land birds and 83 water birds, in all 204 nominal species. No doubt his friend [Andrew] Downs assisted him considerably in the compilation of this list.

Campbell Hardy's drawing of moose hunting at Scraggy Lake, March 1853, served as the front plate for Volume 1 of his *Sporting Adventures in the New World or Days and Nights of Moose-Hunting in the Pine Forests of Acadia.*

"The Bivouac," a sketch of camping at Scraggy Lake, was the front piece for Volume II of *Sporting Adventures in the New World*.

"These racy and well-written sketches of sport and natural history attracted much attention, and soon made their young author well known in England as well as in Canada. His was the first comprehensive account of moose-hunting in this province, the attractions of which had hitherto only been made known in a limited manner by letters from officers on this station. This first work of Hardy is apparently fairly scarce. [First edition two-volume sets sell today for $1,000].

"On 6th June, 1855, he married, in the Garrison Chapel, Halifax, Matilda Sydney Stotherd, eldest daughter of the late Lt. Col. (afterwards General) Richard John Stotherd, C.B., Commanding Royal Engineer on this station, and subsequently Colonel Commandant of Royal Engineers at Dover, England. By this marriage, he had [eight] children …

"On 31st Dec. 1862, he and other kindred spirits, such as J.M. Jones, Thos. Belt, Dr. J.B. Gilpin, Capt. Lyttleton, R.G. Haliburton, and others, were present at the inaugural meeting of the Nova Scotian Institute of Natural Science; and he was elected a member of the first council. Regarding the foundations of the society, he wrote me a few years ago: 'I remember well the friendliness and hearty cooperation of our efforts to set forward the development of local knowledge of the natural history and resources of the province. We were a band of enthusiastic lovers of nature – hunters and woodsmen, zoologists and geologists, botanists and fishermen, historians and antiquarians, each zealous of improvement in his own particular sphere of knowledge or science.'

"At the first ordinary meeting, held 19th Jan. 1863, he read the second paper communicated to the new society, on 'Nocturnal Life of Animals in the Forest' which gives a delightful account of our forest life at night. Then followed each year other papers by him. ... He served as second vice-president from Oct. 1863 to Oct. 1864, and then was first vice-president for three years, till Oct. 1867, he having by that time departed the province. ...

"He was caribou-shooting and salmon-fishing in Newfoundland in the summer of 1863, and returned to Halifax in July. He was an able artist and keenly interested in art, and in Nov. of that year, he, Capt. Lyttleton (a fine artist) and Capt. W. Chearnley brought together a picture exhibition in the drill-room at Halifax, at which he showed his two beautiful water-colours [see page 32 and 33] ..., which had just been engraved in London, and other sketches, principally relating to moose-hunting ...

"In August 1866 he, with an Indian, Glode, journeyed by canoe to Tobiaduc Brook, several miles westward of Lake Rossignal, Queens Co., and made a careful investigation of beaver houses there, from which he constructed two beautiful models with sketch and samples of cuttings, foodsticks and bedding, one of which is in the Provincial Museum, Halifax, and the other he presented to the Zoological Society of London. The Halifax model was shown at the Exposition Universelle, Paris, in 1867, and attracted marked attention. In Dec. 1866 he read an able paper on the Beaver in Nova Scotia. … From time to time he also contributed sporting sketches to *The Field* and *Land and Water*. (From an expression in a lecture of Gen. Hardy, one is led to believe that his last night in our woods was when they camped at the outlet of Lake Rossignol on this expedition.)

These two Campbell Hardy renditions of browsing moose and caribou on the barrens are from his third book, *Forest Life in Acadie,* published in 1869.

Lithographs of Campbell Hardy's watercolours *The Forest Road – Summer* and *The Forest Road – Winter* were published in London June 2, 1863, by Day & Son.

"For five and a half years he had been Inspector of Warlike Stores and Firemaster at Halifax, and subsequently in 1866 and 1867 was Inspecting Officer of the Nova Scotian Militia Artillery. In August 1867, ... he finally left Halifax to return to England, at the age of thirty-six, after fifteen and a half years' residence here. He took with him many trophies of the chase, mounted by Andrew Downs. He always considered his sojourn here as the most eventful and pleasant period in his life, and his mind never ceased to dwell upon the impressions he had then gained.

"With his heart still deep in our pine forests, he published in 1869 in New York, his most familiar work, and the one in which he is at his very best, *Forest Life in Acadie: Sketches of Sport and Natural History in the Lower Provinces of the Canadian Dominion*, with twelve plates, all but one from his pencil, but not done justice to by the engraver. In this delightful volume his style leaves nothing to be desired, for it is a fine literary work apart from its other qualities. It still must rank as the best-written book that has yet appeared on woodland sport in Nova Scotia, and has a charm about it which is derived from the fine character and talents of its author.

Campbell Hardy's sketch of a Nova Scotia lumber camp appeared in his 1869 book *Forest Life in Acadie*. Winter work scenes depicting oxen and log cabins remained relatively unchanged until well into the 1900s.

"The volume contains sketches of the country, of the forests and streams, of the moose and caribou and the hunting of them; careful accounts of the beaver, otter and other important animals, of the fish and the fishing, camping, the progress of the seasons, and other miscellaneous valuable observations on natural history, the nocturnal life of animals in our forest, etc.

"There is an interesting account of a moose hunt with old Joe Cope, about the Big Indian Lake, between the Head of St. Margaret's Bay and Mount Uniacke, also of a caribou hunt, in December, to the north of Parrsborough, and of moose-calling near Beaver Bank, being guided by John Williams on the two last expeditions. Some of the chapters had originally appeared, over the nom-de-plume Alecs in *The Field* and *Land and Water*. He refers frequently under the name of 'The Old Hunter' to that king of local sportsmen, Capt. William Chearnley, whose name is indelibly associated with the history of sport in this province and in after years he carried on an extensive correspondence with Chearnley until the latter's death in July 1871.

Campbell Hardy turned his drawing of a cow and calf moose into a Christmas card.

An idyllic Campbell Hardy scene depicting two wildcats or lynx.

"After leaving Halifax in 1867, he was stationed at Dover, Gibraltar, Chatham, Aldershot and Queenstown. He obtained his majority on 5th July, 1872, and his lieutenant-colonelcy on 16th Jan. 1875, and was promoted to colonel on 16th Jan. 1880, finally retiring on full pay, 29th May, 1880, with the honorary rank of major-general. He then went to pass the concluding years of his life at 3 Victoria Park, Dover, England, and resided in that garrison town until his death. There he took a foremost part in all good works. …

"About 1900 Lord William Seymour told me that General Hardy was still alive and keenly interested in Nova Scotia and our Institute [of Natural Science], and desired to be remembered to some of my family with whom he had been associated in sport. This renewed an acquaintance by correspondence, which evidenced how vivid were all his recollections of those old days. He still cherished an earnest desire to revisit Nova Scotia, to see its forests and rivers, and other well-remembered scenes, his surviving friends and the Indians, and to once more fish and shoot here; but this wish he was not able to gratify. On 30th Oct., 1903, he renewed his connection with the Institute, being elected a corresponding member in consideration of his past services and continued interest, and as being its last surviving original member.

"He lived a rather retired and often invalid life, his health being somewhat broken by a severe attack of influenza in March, 1913. For some years … his work had been almost entirely connected with the topic of nature study and attempts to promote it as a most useful factor in the education of a child's mind. To this end he had yearly gatherings and exhibitions at St. James's Parish Hall, Dover. He also occasionally lectured, and about 1900 delivered a most interesting and instructive address … entitled 'In Evangeline's Land,' which contained vivid descriptions of Nova Scotia, its productions, scenery and sport, and of its Indians and their legends, interspersed with anecdotes.

"Being a talented artist, much of his time was devoted to painting scenes connected with Nova Scotian forests and lakes, their wild life, and the pursuit of sport; and his annual Christmas card was one of his sketches, accompanied by a booklet on some meditative subject. …

"After having been in indifferent health for some months, he passed away on 11th April, 1919, in his eighty-eighth year, but in entire possession of all his faculties, and with still his characteristic sunny boy-like disposition, which made him beloved by everyone who knew him. Up to the very last he wished he could 'go back' to Nova Scotia. The same day died his great friend, Col. Samuel Parr Lynes, R.A., who as a lieutenant in the gunners, had fished and hunted and paddled with him in Nova Scotia in 1857 and 1858, and who corresponded with him regularly."

Dr. Jerry Lonecloud, 1854-1930, (a.k.a. Jeremiah Bartlett, Alexis or Jeremiah Luxey) holds the birchbark cross honoring Campbell Hardy. Born in Maine to Nova Scotia Mi'kmaq parents Mary Ann and Abram, Lonecloud lived an interesting life, widely noted as a Mi'kmaq medicine man, guide and storyteller. His uncle, Tom Philips, part Mi'kmaq, part Acadian, guided for Campbell Hardy.

"Hardy's remains, covered with the nation's flag, on which were his busby and sword, were borne on a six-horse gun-carriage, and laid to rest in a moss- and flower-lined grave in St. James's Cemetery, next to his deceased son. A cross of birch-bark and porcupine-quill work, made by the widow of his favourite Indian guide, John Williams, is appropriately placed to his memory in the parish church.

Left: "Honest" John Williams, the "most expert of Micmac guides," and a favourite of Campbell Hardy. Right: Sportsman Frederick Harris D. Vieth, author of *Recollections of the Crimean Campaign and the Expedition to Kinburn in 1855 including also Sporting and Dramatic Incidents in connection with Garrison Life in the Canadian Lower Province*, 1907. Other British officers who wrote of their sporting adventures while stationed at Halifax were M.M. Hammond (*Memoir of Captain M.M. Hammond, Rifle Brigade*, 1858); Francis Duncan (*Our Garrisons in the West*, 1864); and Richard Dashwood (*Chiploguorgan or Life by the Camp-fire*, 1872).

"… he never lost the spell which Nova Scotia had cast upon him. In fact, he always cherished affection for places and persons with which he had been associated, and never forgot an associate, however humble. His old Micmac guides, the noted John Williams, Joe Cope, Francis Paul, Christopher Paul, and others, were never forgotten and often referred to … The Indian welcome as he paused at the wigwam's entrance, 'Come in, Hardee, bon soul,' echoed sweetly in his ears for fifty years, with the remembrance of the weird night-cry of the loon on the lake, and the spiritual evensong of the hermit thrush.

"He was a keen sportsman of the clean English school, elated by the excitement of the chase but never taking an unfair advantage of an animal. His chief delight was moose-hunting and fly-fishing for salmon and trout. His name will go down in our sporting annals with those of his friend Col. W[illiam] Chearnley, Dr. J.B. Gilpin, Charles Hallock, Lt. Francis Duncan, Dy. Asst. Com. Gen. F.C. Blunt, F.H.D. Vieth, F.W. Blaiklock, Capt. Champagne L'Estrange, Hon. Charles Alexander, E.G. Stayner, Charles Stayner, Dr. B.W.C. Deeble, the erratic Lt. J.M. Macgowan, A.P. Silver, some relatives of my own, and other well known local sportsmen, men of varying temperament, but each with the deep-seated love of clean sport.

Non-Native hunters, like the two Campbell Hardy depicted here, called moose but according to him, "It is in giving vent to the sound, making it appear to come from the lungs of a moose and not from those of a man, that the Indian excels." Moose calling was traditionally done at night during the full moon of the autumn rut in September and October.

"As is often the case with true sportsmen, an intense love of all nature seems to have been very largely at the bottom of Hardy's love for sport and the forest. Sport without its wild surroundings would have been much less attractive to him. Through all his books runs that love of Nature – not for sport alone, but for herself – which was always a power in his life, and remained so till death. His opportunities for studying the habits of animals in the forest were second to none, and he described with rare discrimination and the utmost accuracy what he observed. He was thus an accurate field naturalist, but he had not the skill in drawing up technical descriptions which Dr. J.B. Gilpin possessed. He was rather prejudiced against such popular American writers as [William J.] Long, [Charles G.D.] Roberts and [Ernest] Thompson-Seton, considering them to be "animal romancers" and their writings valueless to the true naturalist. His knowledge of the Indian, his character and his legends, was remarkably thorough.

A dapperly dressed Campbell Hardy, standing centre in civilian clothes, poses with a group of Canadian Boer War soldiers at a convalescent home operated by his daughter Lucy in Dover, England, 1901-02.

"He was an amateur artist of most distinct talent, working in watercolours, oils and pencil, but mostly in the first, and continuing to do so to the very last. As his subjects, he took mostly woodland, lake and river scenery in the wilds of Nova Scotia, and sporting incidents, largely relating to the moose, all most truthfully represented and with distinct artistic skill in composition. ...

"As a writer he possessed a charming, polished style, which lends a literary flavor to his sporting sketches, and makes some of them almost classics in their way. The accounts of his adventures are entirely free from traces of the boastful strain so common in some writers in modern American sporting magazines; and he tells of his failures, as well as his successes, in a manner devoid of egotism. No doubt *Forest Life in Acadie*, his more mature work, shows him at his best. He occasionally essayed poetry, and his unpublished stanzas, 'A Brook of the Northern Woods,' as usual referring to this country, show considerable merit. ..."

Halifax studio portraits of British military personnel in standard issue dress and sporting garb.

As a closing tribute to Campbell Hardy we turn to Paulette Chiasson, the author of "As Others Saw Us: Nova Scotian Travel Literature from the 1770s to the 1860s" (*Nova Scotia Historical Review* Vol. 2, #2, 1982), who wrote, "The only British traveller who came to know the Micmacs at all well was Campbell Hardy. ... His many hunting expeditions with native guides provided him with an excellent opportunity to become acquainted with them, and as a result, he acquired a more sympathetic outlook than most other observers. The stranger, reasoned Hardy, formed his opinion based upon 'what he has heard from unreasonable and prejudiced settlers.' Hardy boldly defended the Indian cause. 'It is the white man who has kept aloof from the Indian, oppressed him, deprived him of his natural means of supporting existence.' Hardy's description of the Micmac was probably the most sympathetic in all the travel literature concerning Nova Scotia. He was aware of the attitudes of white settlers, and rather than write a general criticism of the poverty and intemperance of the native people, his first-hand experiences led him to emphasize their potential and capabilities as individuals. ..."

The Mi'kmaq were Nova Scotia's first tour operators. Guides such as Chief Jim Meuse from Bear River, shown here c.1910 wearing King George III Peace Medals, would have been in demand by sportsmen even at such an advanced age.

The Military Tourist Era came to a close in 1871, "a date chosen with some care" according to Dr. James Morrison, who writes that an event that year "marked the beginning of large scale tourism in Nova Scotia. In July 1871, a large party of some 400 Americans travelled by railroad to Nova Scotia from Boston, becoming the first tourist excursion to travel by rail to the province. By the next summer, rail service was extended to New York, and a 36-hour journey was all that was necessary to travel from the wilds of New York City to the civilized wilderness of Nova Scotia."

The initial influx of tourists was followed by a "promotional campaign" that resulted in travel writers spinning reams of eloquent descriptive prose. "Simple farming communities now became 'picturesque rustic settlements sheltered among the green-robed senators of the mighty woodlands.'" This ushered in the Elite Sport Tourist Era for Nova Scotia (1871-1940), a time in the broader context of history that American writer John Mitchell dubbed "the gilded age of the field sports."

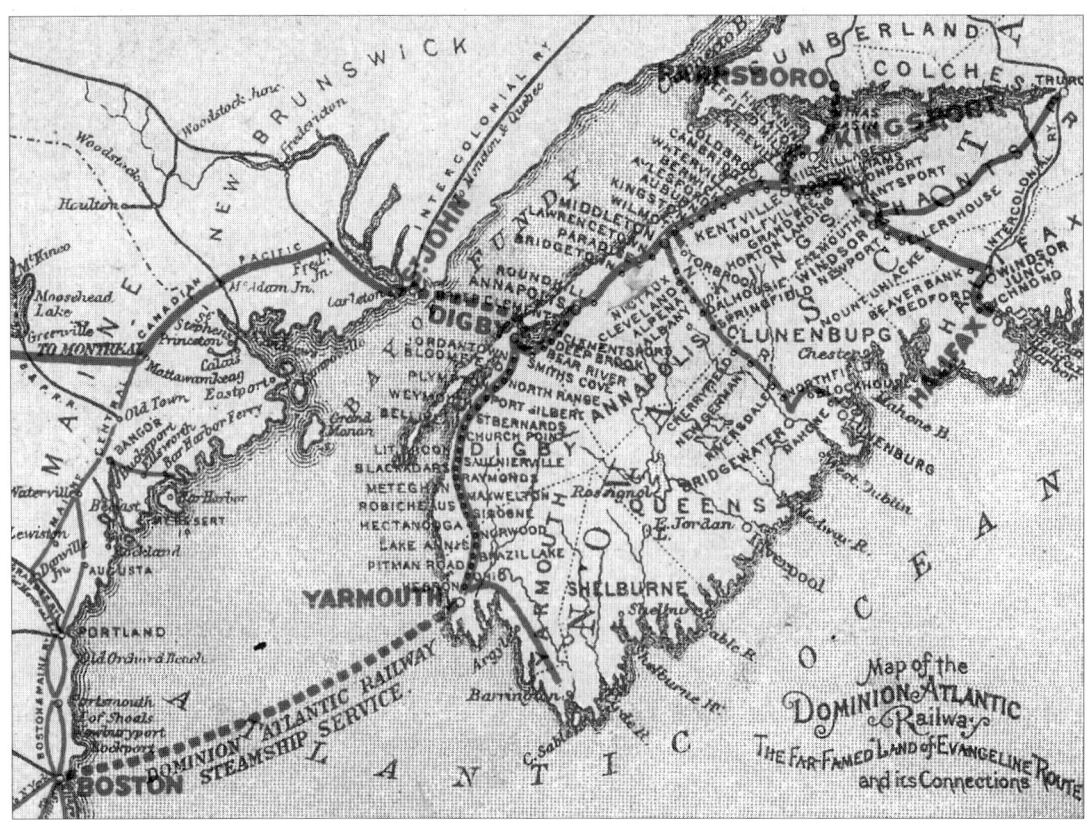

A ferry service connected Boston, Massachusetts, with Digby and Annapolis Royal, Nova Scotia, via Saint John, New Brunswick, as early as the 1830s. By the 1850s a ferry was operating directly between Boston and Yarmouth, Nova Scotia. These two water routes were used extensively by sportsmen from the eastern seaboard of the United States, who flocked to the woods and waters of southwestern Nova Scotia during the Elite Sport Tourist Era.

From the mid-1800s to the turn of the twentieth century, illustrated newspapers such as *Harper's Weekly* and *Frank Leslie's Illustrated* popularized sporting opportunities in Nova Scotia. Artists and writers on special assignment sketched and described a woodland scene "as it was making history," then "rushed" their work off to American east coast publishers where skilled artisans engraved the drawings on blocks of wood for printing. Within a week the public were enthralled by newspaper accounts which today are considered valuable "historically accurate records" as well as "exquisitely engraved works of art."

Late nineteenth and early twentieth century issues of *Forest & Stream* and *Outing* magazines printed articles about moose hunting in Nova Scotia. But according to the provincial chief game commissioner, "Most of the big game hunting here in the province is done by residents, that being done by non-resident sportsmen being negligible and confined to a few sporting centres, for the most part in the western part of the province …"

Three sketches from an article in *Harper's Weekly*, July 20, 1878, entitled "Moose Hunting in Nova Scotia." The title for this sketch is Moose Stalking – The Moose Surprised.

"The idea is prevalent throughout the country that our big game is a great source of revenue to the province from non-residents, American hunters," continued the chief game commissioner's report. "This idea is erroneous. ... The real tourist attraction in Nova Scotia woods is fishing which is indulged in during the months of the summer holidays. Very few people can afford to go hunting in the fall months and only few tourists are sufficiently hardy to sleep outdoors in tents during the cold weather. The moose and for that matter, all the wild game, has much more importance to the province alive on account of the glamour it gives to the woods when seen by the fishermen and tourists."

Back to Camp

The Camp – Moose Steak

Sketches from *Harper's Weekly*, February 21, 1880, illustrating a canoe trip on Lake Rossignol.

A travel article that appeared in *Harper's Weekly* February 21, 1880, entitled "Canoeing in Nova Scotia," described a trip from Kejimkujik through Lake Rossignol to Liverpool. "One great charm in a visit to Nova Scotia lies in the fact that it has never yet been but imperfectly surveyed. There is, so to speak, plenty of room for a moderate amount of novel exploration and discovery. This thought, together with the other attractions of the country, was the one that led a couple of adventurous gentlemen to make the canoe journey, incidents of which are depicted in our sketches. …

"After a journey of over a hundred miles, Liverpool was reached, with clothes and canoes much the worse for wear. There was abundant compensation, however, in renewed health and strength, and the recollection of many pleasant hours passed on the lakes and in the woods. The only real drawback to a journey of this kind is the flies, which in summer give the trout so much satisfaction and human beings so much annoyance. The Indians theory, that, 'If you kill one, thousands come to his funeral,' seems to be perfectly true. …"

Top left: "Protection Against the Flies – Tar Oil And Lots Of It" Top right: "Crossing Lake Rossignol" Bottom: "An Anxious Moment – Running the Rapids – Grub on Board"

Drawings from a *Harper's Weekly* article, "Salmon Fishing in Nova Scotia," December 8, 1877.

Nova Scotia's forests, having not yet experienced the coming devastation wrought by the pulp and paper industry, beckoned non-resident wilderness travellers. Gerry Parker notes in his highly regarded book *Men of the Autumn Woods: Non-Resident Big-Game Hunting in New Brunswick, The Golden Years 1885-1935*, "The land [in the United States] had been virtually stripped of the forests – in many northeastern states as much as three-quarters of the landscape was deforested by the early 1800s."

He quotes sportsman Fred Irland, a bureaucrat from Washington, D.C., who wrote in 1896, "In the United States we have seen the forests melt away like snow in an April wind, and have come to look upon them as merely transitory; so that it is difficult for Americans to realize the extent to which, in the region of earliest European occupation of Canada, primeval conditions endure. In the immediate presence of civilization more than two hundred years old, the wilderness of the Maritime Provinces preserves its perpetual youth. ... The few who have penetrated its depths have found it a veritable land of enchantment."

This picture from the late 1890s is believed to be of an anonymous guide from the Eastern Shore.

By the early 1900s many non-Natives knew well the way of the woods and had taken up guiding, a job that paid a daily wage of two dollars – double the amount earned working in lumber camps. From the time guide licenses were first issued in 1907 until the closing years of the Elite Sport Tourist Era, the majority of licenses were sold in Annapolis County, followed closely by the counties of Queens, Yarmouth, Shelburne and Digby. Some guides worked independently, providing lodging for sportsmen in their homes or at a cabin or tent camp while others were on call for the hotels and lodges that catered to visiting anglers and hunters. Many "sports" arrived in May with steamer trunks packed full with the necessities needed to "stay 'til the cold weather drove them out." Dr. James Morrison writes that for the guides "it was never altogether clear as to why this rich crowd would want to spend $10 a week for board just to sit around an oil lamp in the wilds of Nova Scotia."

Guide Jim McLeod was a popular subject of noted photographer Wallace MacAskill, who took promotional photographs for Nova Scotia tourism in the 1930s, including the one on the right of Jim which was the back cover of a brochure.

"Big" Jim McLeod, far right, whoopin' it up at his camp, Echo Lodge, on the Medway River, Queens County. Guiding tales tall and true abound from the Elite Sport Tourist Era, with none more storied than Jim McLeod; several stories are recounted in *Guides of the North Woods*.

NOVA SCOTIA, OCTOBER, 1919

Men of fame and fortune came to Nova Scotia. American writer Irvin S. Cobb (1876-1944), shown at left in both photos, was a portly, cigar-chomping humorist from Kentucky who visited Annapolis County in October 1919 with an entourage of sportsmen (including Damon Runyon, sports editor for the New York *Tribune*) on a moose hunting trip to Red Lake. Cobb has been compared to Mark Twain and Edgar Allan Poe, with more than 300 published short stories and 60 books, which made him one of the highest paid writers of the early 1900s.

NOVA SCOTIA, OCTOBER, 1919

NOVA SCOTIA, OCTOBER, 1919

Irvin Cobb wrote a lighthearted article in 1926 about his moose hunting adventure in Nova Scotia (see *Where Moose and Trout Abound*) in which he pondered the plural of moose. "If the plural of goose were geese and the plural of mouse were mice, it seemed reasonable to assume that the plural of moose should be mise ..." Local photographer Paul Yates accompanied Cobb on his backwoods foray into Annapolis County and preserved the occasion by printing postcards, four of which are shown here.

NOVA SCOTIA, OCTOBER, 1919

Zane Grey (1872-1939) was another acclaimed writer of the early 1900s who frequented Nova Scotia, fishing both its inland and coastal waters. Here, the Western novelist poses with his 758-pound world-record tuna he caught in 1924 at Jordan Bay, Shelburne County.

A curio from Zane Grey's fishing days along the Nova Scotia coast lies far inland near the mouth of the Shelburne River at Lake Rossignol. His c.1920s fishing boat, repaired and refurbished into a camp at the time of this 1996 photograph, has since fallen on hard times and is now said to be "pretty much done up." Sources believe the vessel eventually became the property of Bowater Mersey Pulp & Paper Co. and was used as a boom boat on Lake Rossignol to move pulpwood.

Baseball legend Babe Ruth attracted a crowd of curious on-lookers at the Yarmouth ferry during his trip home from Nova Scotia following an obviously successful hunting trip to Tusket c.1935.

Many professional athletes hunted and fished in Nova Scotia, one of the more famous being George Herman "Babe" Ruth (1895-1948), baseball's Sultan of Swat. Ruth made several trips to the province in the late 1930s and early 1940s to fish, hunt, golf and attend various social functions. In 1937 he appeared in a tourism movie promoting Yarmouth County and in 1942 gave a hitting demonstration at the Halifax Wanderers Grounds. When Ruth visited the Tusket area of Yarmouth County his guides were Acadian-French woodsmen Peter and Louis Vacon from Quinan.

The Babe was notorious during his baseball playing days for being out on the town until all hours, a reputation he maintained while in Tusket. Legend says that while here, Ruth enjoyed evenings of cards, Jack Daniels and cigars mixed with a plethora of tales told round the campfire. Guides and their charges would eventually retire to the bunks for a couple of hours shut-eye before a dawn wake-up call. Ruth, who required little sleep, would slip outside in the wee hours of the morning and fire both barrels from his Remington shotgun into the air, bringing guides Peter and Louis crashing and cursing to the floor. With a laugh and grin, Ruth would then return to the cabin and begin cooking a 4 a.m. breakfast for everyone while bleary-eyed guides and sportsmen awaited the coming of day.

Henry William Johnstone Bonnycastle Dale (left) and Cecil "Laddy" Griffith on the Clyde River, 1936.

Two interesting non-resident sportsmen were Henry William Johnstone Bonnycastle Dale (1861-1936) and his assistant Cecil "Laddy" Griffith. Both were originally from Ontario, where Cecil began working in 1916 at the age of 10 for Bonnycastle Dale, who was frail and "liked to be waited on." Legend says the Griffith family, which had several children, were friends with the Dale family and when Cecil's father died, Bonnycastle Dale took one of the older boys, Eric, to help out the widow Griffith. When Eric joined the army, Bonnycastle Dale offered to look after Cecil, who then became his long-time caregiver. Griffith cooked meals, did household chores, carried cameras and, later in life, paddled Bonnycastle Dale's canoe.

The "odd couple" eventually settled in the Clyde River area after travelling extensively across Canada. Bonnycastle Dale, a pen name he adopted from his mother's maiden name of Bonnycastle, was an ardent angler, hunter, noted outdoor writer and naturalist, whose articles appeared regularly in *Rod & Gun in Canada* magazine. "Tall, lanky, and formally attired," Bonnycastle Dale lived a simple life, his favorite three possessions being a camera, Model-T and dog. For his part, Griffith worked throughout Shelburne County as a farmer, woodsman, guide, mail carrier and writer, assuming the pseudonym Bonnycastle Dale Jr. following his mentor's death in 1936. The two "loners" are buried in Middle Clyde.

Women too enjoyed roughing it in the deep unknown of Nova Scotia's backwoods. The c.1900 image on the left was taken somewhere in Halifax County. The one on the right shows guide Tom Scott Sr. (left), his son Charlie and an unidentified lady from a fishing party on Barrington River, Shelburne County, c.1910. Promotional literature from the Elite Sport Tourist Era promised "ladies will find life [in Nova Scotia] a novel and delightful experience … Climate perfect. Air crisp and bracing. No fog nor malaria nor hay fever …"

The guide in the left photo would have been a busy man catering to this sizable group of Mayflower Ladies at Spruce Lodge, Hants County, prior to setting out for a day of fishing and picnicking, c.1918. For the less adventurous, there was ample opportunity for shaded strolls along a woodland path, like the one at right at Milford House, Annapolis County.

Promotional photographs of the Elite Sport Tourist Era depicted scenes of camping, canoeing, portaging, fishing and hunting as they happened. Similar advertising efforts during the Mobile Tourist Era, as shown here, had lost the authenticity of earlier days and were almost comical in how contrived a scene they portrayed. It is doubtful if either of these ladies or their "guide" ever spent a night under canvas.

Post-World War II Nova Scotia tourism brochures still promoted fishing and hunting but focused on the province being "a haven ... for motorists, cyclists, picnickers, swimmers, boating enthusiasts, camera fans, artists [and] bird watchers ..."

The Elite Sport Tourist Era waned after World War II as the increased popularity and availability of the automobile ushered in the Mobile Tourist Era, which is continuing today. The tourism potential of the automobile was evident as early as 1922 when 2,000 tourist vehicles entered Nova Scotia in just three months. By 1940 nearly 50,000 out-of-province plates were seen in the province, a number that ballooned to 271,000 by 1969, the majority of those being tourism related. With "touring" the rage, no longer were visitors wanting to pole, paddle and portage the backcountry, nor did they have months of vacation time or the inclination to while away their precious hours reposing on a hotel veranda like the days of yore. Although hunting and fishing still remained popular during the early years of the Mobile Tourist Era, the clientele had noticeably changed. They were now predominately from the middle-class, who – according to one old-time guide – "wanted the most for the least," unlike the wealthy patrons of old who could have had everything but demanded little or nothing.

The author and his father Mal Parker (1913-1980) on Sixth Lake Stream, Digby County, 1959.

Being a child of the Mobile Tourist Era, I was born and raised in Bear River, a tiny village straddling the Annapolis-Digby county lines. Like scores of other Nova Scotia communities, it was built upon lumbering and shipbuilding. Bear River was "a hot point years ago for guiding" and as the "gateway to the interior of southwestern Nova Scotia" it became a mecca for sportsmen entering the Land of the Tent Dwellers.

My father Malcolm (Mal) Parker was born into the Elite Sport Tourist Era and grew up hunting, fishing, trapping and guiding throughout the backcountry of Bear River. Later in life, when the necessity of raising a family dictated a career change to proprietor of the Bear River Trading Company – a country general store selling groceries, hardwares and dry goods – his passion for the woods never waned until the day he died, literally. On more than one occasion Dad said he could think of no better place to die than in the woods. In 1980 he got his wish. After a day of heavy paddling, a couple of drinks and a few hands of cards, Dad went to bed in the camp bunk and never woke up. Just as he wanted it.

Left: The author at six years old and "Teddy," bedtime, Wild Garden Sporting Cabins, Sixth Lake Stream, 1959. Right: Author and older brother Neil enroute to Sixth Lake Stream, 1961.

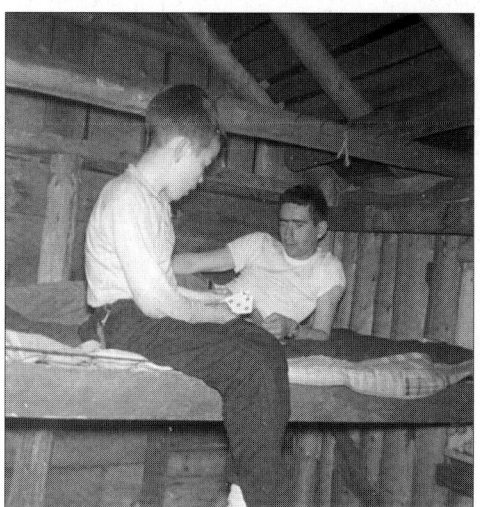 

Left: Author, 10, playing cards with brother Gerry, 20, at Osborne's Camp, White Sand Stream, 1963. Right: Author with sister Mary Lou and father at Osborne's Camp, 1963. In 1930, Mi'kmaq guide Louis Peters from Bear River advertised four cabins at this site. There was only one building habitable when we stayed here in the 1960s.

With Dad's passing came the sudden realization that all the woods stories my brothers, sister and I had grown up hearing many times over at camp, in the store, at home, and in the kitchens of relatives and friends were gone. Not gone from our memories, but gone in the sense they would never be told again in the way that only someone who has lived the life can spin them. Strange the hand fate deals, but had Dad lived another twenty years, I might not have turned down the author's path, as all or most people of his generation interviewed for my first book would have been gone as well.

I then spent four years travelling Nova Scotia with a tape recorder, interviewing the last of the old-time woodsmen whose reminisces and tales formed the basis of my first book, *Guides of the North Woods*, a compilation of oral and written history piecing together the story of Nova Scotia's guiding tradition. Many books have followed but none have been as near and dear to my heart as the first – until now.

Into The Deep Unknown is meant to be a stand-alone book as well as a supplement for Paine's *The Tent Dwellers* and my own *Guides of the North Woods*. The hope is that *Into The Deep Unknown* will find a place in the rucksack and day pack, on the cabin table and coffee table and that it will be browsed and read by the campfire on "the green shores of a Nova Scotia June" and in front of the hearth when "the still places of the North are white and the waters fettered."

Striking out on the Shelburne River, c.1930

Where the trail leads back from the water's edge –
Tangled and overgrown –
Shoulder your load and strike the road
Into the deep unknown.
        – Albert Bigelow Paine, *The Tent Dwellers*

Chapter 1
In The Wake Of The Tent Dwellers
by M.B. Miller, 1911

To the grammarian and purist this letter, laboriously pencilled on a rough sheet of paper and still faintly smelling of the ill-defined but characteristically pungent odors of the lumber camp, was beneath contempt, but to me it was too eloquent of future joys for captious criticism:

> Five Mile River, Febary 10, 1910.
>
> Dear Sir:
>
> Receied your lette to day th 10. I know the partey speeking about. They will hap to go up cowphan, tak a carry and go to hoosehead Lack wich Is the headwaters of Weameth River. And then they Is a streem wich goes to Diwst Lack. When you get to Diwst Lack there is A Lake abot 3 miles father on, and when you get to that Lak there A carry abot 2 mile Long wich will carey you to Oakland Lack. they Is A carey between 5 Lack and Moosehed Lak no good to goe that carey for It about 4 Miles Long and you will lose A lot of fishing If you go that way. Come and we can tak you though safety and hap a plenty fishing. I will be home the 10th of March.
>
> Yours Truley
Louis

As I laid the letter down the busy, nerve-exhausting life of the great city faded away; once again I faintly heard the weird cry of the loon across the lake, the lap-lap of the clear dark waters against the canoe; and as in fancy I drew into my lungs the crisp, balsam-scented Nova Scotian air, innumerable vistas of the wilderness, the real wilderness, flashed through my mind and the yearning to go back to it gripped me with overpowering force. Practically, this rough scrawl meant the realization of a dream which had beset my vagrant thoughts for many weeks – a chance to go deeper into the woods than ever before and particularly to attempt with a fair warranty of success to make the trip from the Lake Rossignol waters over the headwaters to Oakland Lake and thence down the Tusket to the sea.

Famed Mi'kmaq guide Louis Harlow and his wife Madeline, early 1900s. For most of the year they lived in a "rough camp" near Milford House, Annapolis County, where Louis guided sportsmen and Madeline crafted baskets for tourists. They spent winters at the First Nations Reserve in the village of Bear River. Their two sons Jim and Charlie would eventually join Louis in the guiding profession.

The "Louis" of my letter was Louis Harlow, a Micmac Indian, an excellent guide and expert canoeman, who had hunted and trapped over much of the territory in question and his assurance that the plan was feasible settled many doubts. The only part left for us was to complete our arrangements and await the chosen time.

In the spring of the year before [1909], our party of four had visited familiar haunts on the Upper Tusket, then returning to the railroad had journeyed several hours to Annapolis Royal. Crossing South Mountain a drive of sixteen miles had landed us at South Milford on one of the Milford chain of lakes. Here we were greeted and welcomed by that famous man of the woods, A.D. Thomas, the genial "Dell" of Albert Bigelow Paine's *Tent Dwellers*, who was ready to outfit us and send us on our way through the Nova Scotian wilderness to Liverpool on the Atlantic seaboard.

With Charles Charleton, Lawrence Munro and two Indians, Louis Harlow and David Gloade as guides, and in four canoes, we made a never-to-be-forgotten journey of six days down nature's beautiful waterways to the sea. The tale of that adventure need not be told here. We had gone through Lakes Keejeemacoojee and Great Rossignol to the Indian Gardens and on down the rushing Mersey to quaint old Liverpool, but there still remained beyond our ken much which had held our absorbed interest – lakes and streams which seldom were touched by visiting sportsmen, further places which only an occasional trapper reached in his quest for fur, and still beyond was the upland country in which only Indians knew the ancient routes of their forefathers by water and trail. Stern duty did not permit of further

Louis Harlow demonstrates the art of poling a canoe. Only the most skilled woodsmen had the prowess to battle rapids while standing.

Louis Harlow, with birchbark horn, and Del Thomas – Del the Stout from *The Tent Dwellers* – camped at the base of a "calling rock." An expert moose caller, Louis would send out the plaintiff, amorous call of a cow moose through the horn while standing on top of the rock (which amplified the sound and gave a clear field of vision), hoping to entice a rutting bull within shooting distance.

Milford House guide Charlie Charleton (right), the diminutive Charles the Strong immortalized by Albert Bigelow Paine in *The Tent Dwellers*.

wanderings. Our time was nearly up. We could only listen to the stories of our guides as we kept to our way and promise ourselves that maybe, in another year –

Another year had come, and before the slowly returning sun had begun to break the icy fetters of winter, a letter full of inquiries and outlining a tentative plan was dispatched to the helpful Dell. Soon came back an encouraging reply and enclosed was the letter which I have quoted. True, the trip had never been made before, but there was no reason why we should not succeed. There would doubtless be difficulties to surmount, and possibly some hardships, but that was only to be expected. At intervals other letters were exchanged as some suggestion would occur, some important point required elucidation, or some question had to be determined. Similar trips had taught the wisdom of endeavoring to leave nothing to chance, and, as far as possible, to arrange all details beforehand, but finally all that could be reasonably anticipated had been decided.

Close to the time of our departure we had learned with considerable regret that Charlie and Louis could not accompany us, but Lawrence was to go, and with him we were to have two guides, both new to us, but each warmly recommended by our friend Thomas.

This year there could be only three in our party, the fourth companion on our former pilgrimage being sadly situated. His wife and debutante daughter had decreed, with the charming despotism of American women, that European travel would have to be substituted for his usual spring outing for trout. His sentiments on the subject were partially indicated when he remarked one day, with some emphasis, that he had just put $5,000 into a letter of credit and $1,000 more into negotiable checks and he would turn all this over to any fellow who would take his family abroad and let him go with us.

The rest of us were all doctors – two surgeons and one medical man, all close friends and mutually congenial. Gurney, the youngest, albeit not too young, was a fashionable practitioner with a large and exacting clientele, whose demands, however, did not prevent his superabundant energies finding plenty of outlets in various social and business interests. He had had no inconsiderable experience as a fisherman, having caught salmon, trout and ouananiche in Newfoundland, Canada, Nova Scotia, Maine and Wisconsin. He was our official man-at-arms, carrying our only deadly weapons, a .25-caliber pistol; and a camera.

George, the eldest, but not too old, was a surgeon of recognized ability, dextrous and sound in his chosen work, sober and steady by temperament, but entirely too self-deprecatory and modest. A life devoted to winning his way in the world had left but little for extensive outings, so that he had enjoyed his first real experience in the North Woods the previous year. Like the rest he was an enthusiastic and skilled fisherman, but his piscatorial degree had been acquired in the college of salt-water fish.

Finally there was the scribe. Enough may develop in his narrative sufficiently to acquaint the reader with him, but at the onset he is going to confess, and to confess brazenly and without apologies, that there are certain months early in each year in which he practices surgery mainly for the chance it affords him to respond to the call of the red gods. On this venture he was of some presumed value, since he had visited Nova Scotia for several years and was familiar with the Tusket River portion of the trip. Perhaps for this reason it was agreed that he should act as manager, treasurer and general chronicler.

More than two dozen Mi'kmaq and non-Native guides were available for hire in the Milford area. Only two of the four guides in this photo are identified – Ritson Longmire with basket at left and Homer Vidito, on the right. The gentleman with hands on hips is undoubtedly a "sport."

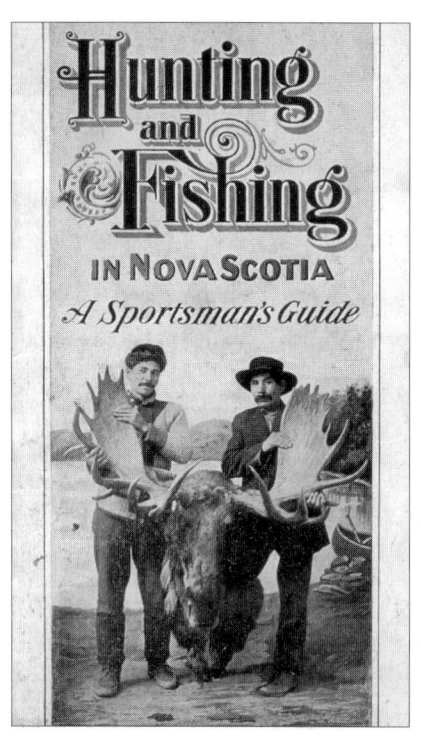 

Mi'kmaq guide Joe Pictou (right) and his son Philip Paul posed for the cover of a c.1915 brochure, which featured 50 pages listing guides, hotels, game laws, licensing fees and sporting opportunities by county. The Dominion Atlantic Railway, which played an instrumental role in promoting early tourism in southwestern Nova Scotia, produced the c.1927 brochure on the right.

On the night of May 19, 1910, the Federal Express rushed Bostonward through the night, carrying our small party over the first stage of the journey. Boston doubtless means divers things to different people, but to us it is the one place on the American continent where a semi-sacred function may be performed with due ceremony and suitable material. I refer to the gastronomic delight of eating broiled live lobster, at the very least a large one, with "fixins," per man. Do not scoff, gentle reader, or imagine that we are sodden gourmands, but take our word for it that nothing can approach this delectable crustacean as a pre-eminently sound foundation for a successful fishing trip to Nova Scotia.

No misanthropy was ever born which can withstand it, no lingering pessimism can overcome its gentle influence, it nestles tenderly and lovingly up to the solar plexus, its delicate colors of scarlet and pink and white inevitably tinge the point of view in similar warm lines, and even though the worst befalls in the subsequent crossing from Boston to Yarmouth and the mighty god Neptune demands his tribute, accept our assurance that there is no form of *mal-de-mer* so mild and indeed almost pleasant as that arising, or rising, from broiled live lobster.

That we did not include it as a course in the breakfast we dispatched directly after our arrival merely indicates that we are men of self-restraint and had due regard for the feelings of the waiter. However, after a morning devoted to shopping for the few things which had been forgotten, to a few calls, and to some other matters of minor importance, we joyously fore-gathered with the lobster.

Our intrepid travellers would have arrived at Boston's South Union train station on Summer Street near the waterfront, which provided easy access for passengers connecting with the ferry service to Nova Scotia. Opened January 1, 1899, it handled as many as 740 trains a day.

By 1 o'clock we and our belongings were safely aboard the *Prince George*, which shortly afterward pulled out from Long Wharf and started down the busy and ever beautiful harbor. In Captain McKinnon and in the purser, Mr. Smith, we greeted old friends who spared no effort to make us perfectly comfortable. As a native Nova Scotian, the captain has a sympathetic appreciation of the merits and shortcomings of sportsmen, and for us it is always an especial pleasure to cross with him. He has a fine fund of quiet anecdote and story for the chosen few who are the recipients of his hospitality in his own cabin. He hails from Chebogue, a little coastal town a few miles from Yarmouth on the south shore. Once in response to my question as to what the people in Chebogue did for a living the chief engineer, a blue-eyed youngster whose Scotch burr was inimitable, beat the captain out for a reply and said: "When business gets dull they tie a lantern to the old cow's neck and turn her out on the beach on stormy nights." [A reference to wreckers who lured ships to their doom with false lights.] The captain's earnestness in repelling this calumny on his fellow townsmen was almost as funny as the original remark.

The trip to Yarmouth was pleasantly uneventful, as the sea was smooth and the weather delightfully warm and clear. We read and mooned and napped the afternoon away, soothed and rested by the soft salt air and the easy roll of the *Prince George*. During the evening Major Dodds, of the Royal Artillery of Montreal, sat late with us in the smoking room swapping tales of the out-of-doors. He had had many interesting adventures afield and afloat in the North Woods, knew the ways of the wild thoroughly, and told his stories admirably.

The arrival of the Boston ferry at Yarmouth.

    The next morning but little was seen of the rock-girdled harbor of Yarmouth, since we were scarcely up at 6 o'clock before the *Prince George* quietly stopped at the wharf. A hasty breakfast and we were ready to go ashore. A brief interview with the Canadian custom officials who passed our dunnage without comment, save to cheerily wish us the best of luck; another interview with the deputy fish warden who, with the adroitness of long practice, parted each of us almost painlessly from a five dollar note for the fishing license, and we had complied with all needful requirements. We then stowed good clothes and suit cases at a convenient checking room, thereafter to depend only upon those marvelous carry-alls, the duffle bags.
    The Nova Scotians are a wholesome people, more hospitable and kindly disposed toward the citizens of the great Republic than the inhabitants of any other section of Canada, save perhaps the Northwest portions. The social and business relations between the Maritime Provinces and the United States are very close, apparently closer than those between some of the Provinces, and these would be even more intimate were it not for tariff walls on both sides of the line. But it is presumptuous to attempt to describe the people of this section by meager generalizations; it is far better to make it a strictly personal matter and say that we frankly like them, that we have never been treated with incivility, nor have we ever been imposed upon in Nova Scotia.
    Yarmouth is a charming old town of about 7,000 inhabitants, resembling in many respects some of the old New England seaports, and like these has seen its growth checked by the substitution of steam for sails. Its very lack of hustle and bustle and push, its quiet repose are strongly commendable features to the weary citizen from the States seeking health, rest or recreation. The arrival of the boat from Boston is still an event worthy of the personal at-

Main Street, Yarmouth.

tention of nearly all the urchins in town, to say nothing of a representative gathering of their elders.

As I have intimated, nothing hurries in Yarmouth; at least, nothing obviously hurries. The "Flying Bluenose Express" was backed down to the wharf where it deliberated delightfully over getting off, even after all the passengers, mail and express parcels were safely stowed away. Finally it crawled in leisurely fashion up through the lower town, past the wooden warehouses and the dilapidated frame houses to the main station, again to pause long enough for the most lingering farewells. Then we were off for the eighty-five mile run to Annapolis, a four-hour trip.

Shortly after leaving Yarmouth the neat and generally pretty farmhouses, each embellished with its regularly spaced orchard, disappeared; then followed mile after mile of monotonous scenery nearly to Weymouth. In the main the prospect showed a dreary succession of low hills, closely strewn with black rocks and covered with a thick heathery growth of bushes, interspersed with swampy hollows filled with thickets of scrubby evergreens. Considering the liberality with which the engineers of the railroad had distributed wondrous curves and still more remarkable grades, the time made by the train was not bad. Generally it seemed as though we were either laboriously pulling up a grade or gloriously coasting down the corresponding slope.

Every four or five miles we came to a station, usually a small wooden building of absolutely no pretensions, with perhaps a store and one or two houses in sight. The names of some of these places were sonorous and attractive Hebron, Hectanooga, Meteghan, Belliveau but as a rule a single glance was quite sufficient. At Brazil Lake we were agreeably surprised to catch a glimpse of our old guide on former outings, Heman Crowell, who had driven sixteen miles from East Kemptville that morning. A frantic waving of hats and hands had to suffice for present greetings, but we knew we were to see him more satisfactorily three weeks later as we came down the Tusket.

As the railroad approached the upper end of Saint Mary's Bay near Weymouth, the scenery improved somewhat, and the hills became more rolling. Here good views were obtained of the tidal Sissyboo, the headwaters of which we were to visit, as we crossed on a high trestle and ran for a short distance parallel to and high above it on the hill. Further on at the pretty town of Digby came the first glimpse of that superb arm of the Bay of Fundy, the far-famed Annapolis Basin. For twenty miles we skirted its southern shores, enjoying a constant succession of magnificent land and water scenes, and realizing very fully what a wonderful setting nature had given to the many dramas history has played on the shores. Near to Annapolis Royal the land was better cultivated and more pastoral, and the blossoming orchards in every direction reminded us that we were entering the garden of Nova Scotia where, it is claimed, the best apples in the world are grown.

Annapolis, the Port Royal of the French period, is a charming, rambling village, faintly reminiscent of rural England, delightfully situated on the upper and narrower part of Annapolis Basin, full of interesting historical associations, and possesses a quaint and picturesque quality of its own which strongly tempts the visitor to tarry long within its environs. We were met at the station by Mr. Thomas' man with the three-seated buckboard and proceeded at

The Goodwin Hotel in Weymouth was patronized by American sportsman in the early 1900s when hunting and fishing the backcountry of Digby County. Hotels like the Goodwin depended on local woodsmen to be at their beck and call to guide parties at a moment's notice.

Enroute to the deep unknown.

once to the Queen's Hotel and had a good dinner, then tried to buy the chocolate for the trip. The diet of the woods is apt to excite a craving for sweets, and we have found that nothing meets this need better, or carries more conveniently in pack or pocket than cakes of pure chocolate. Unfortunately, Annapolis was out of chocolate that day and we were obliged to take in its place maple sugar, later to find it was a fair substitute edibly, but more liable to gather moisture.

It was a sixteen-mile drive in the buckboard to South Milford. The welcome which greeted us at the Milford House was sincere and unaffected, and immediately after supper we went into executive session with Mr. Thomas. We learned that according to instructions the three guides, canoes and equipment had gone ahead that day and would be ready for us on the morrow somewhere below Maitland. We also learned with some chagrin that our expectations of being pioneers in making a trail from Lake Rossignol to the Tusket were doomed to disappointment.

According to Mr. Thomas no one had ever attempted this trip prior to this year, but just ten days ahead of us were two Bostonians, with Charlie Charleton and Louis Harlow as guides, with the same purpose in view. But when we were told what excellent sportsmen they were, and that one of them was a brother in the healing art, and further that the contemplated routes would coincide only as far as Fifth Lake, all feeling of annoyance disappeared. Their party was going on down the Sissyboo as far as Second Lake, and from there get over into the Barrio branch of the Tusket River, while our plan would take us from Fifth Lake up to Sporting Lake and thence to the Oakland Lake headwaters of the Tusket.

The Milford House Express carrying guests' dunnage and supplies leaves Annapolis Royal on the Mooseland Trail, the 70-mile-long former stage coach route between Annapolis Royal and Liverpool that passed "through some of the finest hunting and fishing lands in Nova Scotia." Ox teams and buckboards were replaced in later years by trucks and automobiles.

Mr. Thomas submitted to us the list of provisions he had provided for the trip. To our inexperienced eyes there seemed to be sufficient to last a month, but he informed us that there was only enough for six men for about a fortnight, and the canoes could not safely carry much more. Fortunately the problem of replenishing the food supply had been considered and a letter was sent to our old guide, Heman Crowell at Kemptville, instructing him to send to his camp at Bartlett's eight or ten miles down the Tusket from Oakland Lake and seven miles back from his place, enough food to last the party until we reached the settlements, and to have it there by June 4, two weeks hence.

An hour was passed profitably and pleasantly with Dr. Edward Breck, author of *The Way of the Woods* and other interesting books and essays. Dr. Breck, like the sensible man he is, each year spends as many months as he possibly can either in or on the edge of the wilderness, and for several years he has made his summer home at Milford. We freely discussed with him our proposed adventure, and acting on his advice, concluded to modify our original plan in so far as to leave out the Indian Gardens. To visit them would probably mean that we would be there on the 24th of May, the Queen's birthday, or, as it has been called since the death of Queen Victoria, Empire Day, a day which every good Nova Scotian devotes to fishing, and therefore we might be bothered by undesirable company at such a well-known and popular spot.

Dr. Edward (Eddie) Breck was "a man of many talents" who spoke five languages – serving as a writer for several publications including *The New York Times* and New York *Herald*; vice consul general to Berlin; assistant to U.S. naval attaché in Lisbon; champion fencer for sword, épée and sabre; champion golfer of Germany and Austria; a spy in the Spanish-American War; carried out clandestine operations during World War I in Brazil and Argentina; avid outdoorsman; prolific writer who promoted Nova Scotia tourism in the early 1900s. He was the central character "Eddie" in Albert Bigelow Paine's *The Tent Dwellers*. (For more on Milford House and Eddie Breck see Photo Album I, beginning on page 91).

Milford guide Lawrence (Hod) Munro.

The next morning a jolly but properly subdued party – it being Sunday – left the Milford House before the dew was off the grass and drove the seventeen miles to Roger's Landing. Here awaiting us were the guides and loaded canoes, all prepared for the start. We warmly greeted Lawrence Munro as an old friend who had helped pilot us to Liverpool the year before [1909], and shook hands with the two strange guides, Horace Munro and Charles Sullivan. The two Munros were from Milford and knew the section we were to traverse as far as the upper Shelburne. Sullivan belonged in Weymouth and was familiar with the Sissyboo waterways up to Sporting Lake, while it was tacitly understood that the Scribe was to act as head guide on the Tusket from Oakland Lake to Kemptville.

After lunching *al fresco* in the shade of the great old hemlocks we bade farewell to Mr. Thomas and watched him disappear up the road, then setting up our rods and each selecting a paddle, we stepped into the canoes and pushed off for the long anticipated and fondly hoped-for trip, ready and willing to take whatever fortune the red gods sent. First we paddled out the little brook in the main river, then there followed a half mile of easy going with the current, till presently we rounded a sweeping turn and ran out on to the dancing waves of Lake Keejeemacoojee.

"We stepped into the canoes and pushed off for the long anticipated and fondly hoped-for trip."

Looking out onto Kedgemakooge Lake from the verandah of Kedgemakooge Rod & Gun Club at Jim Charles Point. Clarence Will Mills from Annapolis Royal opened a private resort here in 1906 for wealthy American sportsmen. A detailed account of the club appears in *Guides of the North Woods*.

Keejeemacoojee, Keegeemacoojic, or Kedgemakooge, [Kejimkujik today] as it is variously spelled in the attempts to put the Micmac pronunciation into English, or Fairy Lake – as it is sometimes called – is a magnificent sheet of water, broken by beautiful bays and headlands, and dotted with picturesque islands. Next to Rossignol it is the largest lake in the Province, being fifty-four square miles in area. The significance of the Micmac name is the origin or source of a great river. Its virgin forests of beech and birch, oak and maple have been preserved in their primeval loveliness from the ravages of the lumberman's axe by the fortunate circumstance that from earliest times the bordering lands and many of the islands have been held as Indian grants. Through the decimation and wandering habits of the descendants of the original occupants, the old camping grounds have for many years been deserted and only recently the Government decided to lease the lands and to apply the rentals for the benefit of the remaining tribesmen. It has happened that this lease fell into the hands of C.W. Mills, of Annapolis Royal, who has organized a club to take over the privileges and to preserve the whole section in its natural beauty. [Nothing but pictures remains of Kedgemakooge Rod & Gun Club today, as the lodge and cabins were torn down in the early 1960s with the establishment of Kejimkujik National Park.]

Original 1909 Rod & Gun Club, burned 1916.

Second clubhouse: built 1916, torn down c.1964.

Clubhouse lobby.

Clubhouse dining room.

In addition to a 12-bedroom main lodge there were also 25 cabins for members and guests.

Guides gathered on the Pay Office verandah.

Kedgemakooge Lake was a hub of activity.

An American sportsman poses in front of Jim Charles' Rock, 1899. Jim Charles (c.1830-1905) was a Mi'kmaq guide who c.1860 lived on a point of land which now bears his name in Kejimkujik National Park. According to legend, Jim's notoriety began in the 1870s when he discovered gold. As news spread, Jim was threatened by a white man, Ben Hamilton. In self-defense, Jim killed Hamilton with a blow to the head. Fearing for his life in the white man's court or at the hands of vigilantes, Jim hid out for two or three years in a cave under a large rock deep in the wilds of southwest Nova Scotia, until he was exonerated in absentia of any wrongdoing. Many have searched unsuccessfully for Jim's rock, some claiming it's the one pictured here. Others say this is Jim Charles' Calling Rock he used for moose hunting and that his "hide-out rock" is located nearby. But like Jim's long-lost gold mine, his rock may forever remain a mystery as well.

We paddled out on this superb body of water near Jim Charles Point, a fine level peninsula where there once lived a famous old Indian of that name while further on were the Fairy Rocks, soft sandstone boulders rising sheer from the water's edge. Close to these was the narrow opening of the original Fairy Lake of the Indians, a name which has been applied by the whites erroneously to the larger lake. Across the water to the westward we saw Indian Point, the end of the tongue of land three miles long which projects deeply into the northern end of the lake, and on top of this high promontory was the new club house.

Still further to the westward, island after island stretched away until lost in the distant haze. On that side in the northwest corner empties the Middle River, which has its origin in the chain of lakes of which Frozen Ocean is the largest, while further south is the mouth of the West River, and still further south on the western shore is the trail to Pescawees.

Some believe this large boulder on the shoreline of Sand Beach Lake could be the Jim Charles' Rock of folklore, because it has a small, naturally occurring cave-like enclosure and would have provided a clear field of vision for the fugitive to spot his pursuers – had they ever come.

Old-timers would have disagreed with this being Jim Charles' Rock. Louis Peters, a Mi'kmaq, claimed in the 1930s it was in the barrens, not by the water's edge. Following Louis's lead, Bear River guide Watson Peck spent years scouring the backcountry for the elusive landmark. Finally, in 1967, the November 4 edition of the Halifax *Chronicle Herald* claimed in a front page story "Search For Rock Over." Accompanied by a large photo of Watson sitting atop his new-found granite hideaway, the dogged woodsman reported the discovery to be several miles beyond where others said the rock had been, and that it stood out like a two-storey house. More fuel for the Jim Charles legend.

Lawrence Munro (centre) hitches a ride across "Kedgy" (Kejimkujik) Lake.

Our course took us down the eastern side of the lake past the three Meuse Islands and Peter Glode's Island to the outlet, eight miles. On our trip the year before we had been towed down the lake by a motor boat belonging to the club, but this year there were no adventitious aids in sight, so we turned to with the paddles and woke up some long unused muscles. The outlet is fairly broad and divided by a long narrow island into two channels, and from there to Lake Rossignol is supposed to be twelve miles. Here the current was moderately swift, and as we were tired of paddling, we turned to fishing, George taking the east channel and Gurney and I the west, while the guides merely kept the canoes floating straight with the current and occasionally snubbing them at a favorable spot.

Rather to our surprise, as we had done nothing through this stretch on the previous trip, we commenced to catch trout, not very many and none very large, but still trout, and before we stopped for the night George had taken sixteen, Gurney thirteen and the Scribe eleven. One of Gurney's had risen to the fly with part of a six-inch lamprey eel hanging out of its mouth. Beyond George's Run, where we started fishing, came George's Lake, then the Eelweir and Hemlock Run with more fishing, and then came Loon Lake and the end of the day's run.

"On our trip the year before [1909] we had been towed down the lake by a motor boat ... but this year there were no adventitious aids in sight."

Lewis Glode, a Mi'kmaq, guided for Milford House. "To make our own camp where others had previously camped was a rule we followed ..., as there were many advantages in so doing."

Below Loon Lake outlet are the Loon Lake Falls, with nothing very formidable about them but still requiring a short carry. As the sun was halfway down the western sky, and as it was our first day out, we decided to kill the proverbial two birds with one stone and stop for the night at an old campsite a few feet back from the noisy, tumbling water.

To make our own camp where others had previously camped was a rule we followed whenever we conveniently could, as there were many advantages in so doing, and the disadvantages were trivial and largely involved the esthetics. We were thereby quite sure of a smooth place for the tents and a fire-place with perhaps some charred embers to help start the fire; sometimes a tent pole or two and certainly stakes were available, together with odds and ends which might come in handy; all aids in expediting and making easy our tent dwelling while the mental distress arising from the tin cans and other unlovely debris littered over the fair face of nature was not so very material, especially when one remembered, quite prosaically, that the insects, birds and little animals of the woods are perfect scavengers. At this place we had the unwonted luxury, not to be repeated for many days, of eating our meals at a real table, with accompanying seat, neatly fashioned out of slim birch poles, by some fastidious predecessor.

Four Milford guides enjoy "the unwonted luxury of eating ... meals at a real table, with accompanying seat."

Left to right are Milford guides Charlie Munro, Charlie Charleton, Horace Munro and Howard Germain.

Our supper that night consisted of trout fried to a turn and served piping hot, great mealy potatoes cooked in their jackets, tomatoes stewed with broken bits of ship biscuit, excellent cocoa in the agateware cups, with a sweetener at the end in the form of orange marmalade. Perhaps the bald recital of this menu may not arouse any enthusiasm from the jaded disciple of Lucullus, but for us that night, or indeed thereafter, no foreign chef could have provided more acceptably than did our cook. Of course, the sharpened zest born of long hours afloat in the canoe or afoot on the hike played its part in our enjoyment of Horace [Munro]'s culinary efforts, but beyond all this there could be no denying that he was an excellent and resourceful cook.

In connection with camp cooking, camp food and the appetite which goes with them, a word of caution may be given for the guidance of the unwise or unexperienced. The food which can be carried on a long trip in canoes, or for that matter on pack horses, is rather heavily nitrogenous and lacks the bulky, diluting qualities ordinarily given to a diet by green vegetables. Invariably the active, open air life develops the keenest kind of an appetite, so that the temptation is very strong to over-eat and, what is far worse, to eat too rapidly. Hence, with this sort of food, it frequently happens that the full enjoyment of the first few days is marred by indigestion. To eat slowly, to talk aplenty over meals, and, to drink freely of water, will avoid practically all digestive unhappiness.

"With the set pole either one could probably have surmounted the entire rapids, but with the paddle it was different."

After the evening meal, Horace and Lawrence each took a canoe and gave us an exhibition of paddling up the falls against the current. With the set pole either one could probably have surmounted the entire rapids, but with the paddle it was different. By almost herculean effort and by taking advantage of every swirl and eddy, first one and then the other would climb the torrent inch by inch, but sooner or later the little craft would succumb to the rush of the water and fall back to the pool below.

The long twilight had not faded into night before we were safely tucked away. The absence of evergreens in the neighborhood meant that we slept pretty close to mother earth, and as it became almost frosty during the night, one of our tent mates assured us that there were nothing but rocks in his bed. But we all slept well enough for the first night and woke up at five o'clock refreshed. It was a cool, gray morning with a thick fog blowing softly up the river from the south, but later the fog lifted and the sun shone in our faces as we paddled out on the river.

The day was one to linger in our memories. The Keejeemacoojee River was at its best stage and mood, softly rippling in the light southerly breeze through long reaches of still water, or running at quickened rate in shallower places, where we caught glimpses of the streaming eel grass on the clean rocky bottom, or yet again indulging in falls and rapids to add a spice of apparent danger, as we slid down the slope of curling, foaming white water. The river banks were unblemished by human disfigurements, the trees and bushes in their freshest spring leafage, while overhead a sun-flooded blue sky furnished lights and shades of marvelous loveliness as we meandered, care-free and happy, down the stream.

"All day long we caught gamy hard-fighting trout. At the head and foot of every bit of running water were the speckled trout lying await in the clear dark water for the drop of the fly."

And all day long we caught gamy hard-fighting trout. At the head and foot of every bit of running water were the speckled trout lying await in the clear dark water for the drop of the fly. Sometimes they would rise to the carelessly dangling and trolling flies while we paddled through quiet still waters, and always were we able to get them while running the swifter water of the rapids, provided, of course, that the guide could snub the canoe long enough to permit a cross-current cast.

And it was such sociable fishing – no need to cautiously stalk the likely places, no need to curb any exuberance of spirits or to subdue expressions of joy. What we did not catch might stay and welcome – and anyhow, the ones we took went back. A more nicely devised little river, the Keejeemacoojee, for three anglers could not be imagined, as we could always be close enough to the other fellow to see what he was doing, and many times we fished three abreast. Besides, there was so much room overhead that no fear of a backcast lodging in over-hanging trees bothered us for a moment. Our total catch was 140 trout, and two baby salmon.

We made only eight miles that day. Even the names of the places of interest sounded attractive – Black Rattle, Squaw Camp Brook, Pescawess Stillwater, Pescawess Ledges, Whaleback, Arthur's Ledges, Big Boom, and finally Trout Rock, where our fine little river lost its identity in the broad surface of Lake Rossignol. Of course, we had adventures. Eight shelldrakes were stirred up one by one during the day, and once a black duck flew out from a thicket in evident dismay. We searched for the nest we suspected she had jumped from, but could not find it.

At another place further on a turn in the river brought into view a great owl sitting on a dead tree close to the water's edge. Immediately, Gurney, who had the only firearm, was seized with a desire to slaughter that owl, and while the guide maneuvered the canoe he proceeded to get his gun. First he felt in his hip pocket – it was not there. Then he recalled it was in the pocket in his khaki jacket, and that article of attire was stowed away in the waist of the canoe. Presently he got it out – to find it unloaded and the cartridges somewhere in his duffle bag – and the duffle bag securely locked up. Meanwhile, the owl was perfectly serene, and after a thorough survey of the highly agitated gentleman beneath him, he unconcernedly flew off up the river. But Gurney had some compensation in catching the record fish that day, a nice one weighing a pound and three-eighths.

Packing a firearm year-round was common in the woods before the era of gun registries. Tom Scott, a guide from Barrington, Shelburne County, has a revolver strapped to his hip.

Two unidentified Milford guides take a smoke break while a third enjoys some target practice. Even The Tent Dwellers carried a gun. "We had shooting matches, almost daily," writes Albert Bigelow Paine, "one canoe against the other, usually at any stop we happened to make." All three men are wearing long-sleeved tops (one is rolled up) and pants well tucked into their socks to deter blackflies and mosquitoes – the bane of the north woods.

Photo Album 1
The Tent Dwellers

Bear River photographer and avid outdoorsman Ralph Harris, right, experimented with night photography in the early 1900s, a skill he mastered if this picture is any indication.

MILFORD HOUSE

A. D. THOMAS, - Proprietor.

SOUTH MILFORD, - Annapolis County, N. S.

Telephone Connection with Annapolis Royal.
Bathrooms with Hot and Cold Water. TERMS MODERATE.

THE MILFORD HOUSE with its log cabins is pleasantly situated on the head waters or lakes of the Liverpool or Mersey River, only 15 miles from Annapolis Royal. Good trout fishing, boating, canoeing, bathing, tennis courts, etc. **Good supply of pure spring water.** Parties can start from these lakes and cruise to Kee-gie-ma-kodgie or Fairy Lake, Rossignol, Indian Gardens and Liverpool, also within easy reach of west branch Port Medway, Jordan, Roseway, Lequille and Bear River. All these streams abound in trout. Milford is the starting point to the best shooting places in the province for large and small game. A. D. Thomas' mail team leaves Annapolis Royal after arrival of trains.

PRIVATE TEAMS SUPPLIED BY GIVING NOTICE.

REFERENCES GIVEN IF REQUIRED.

1909 advertisement.

Milford House, originally known as Halfway House then as the Thomas Hotel, was operated by Abraham Thomas in the 1860s as a stagecoach stop on the road running between Annapolis Royal and Liverpool. After his son Adelbert (Del) Thomas took over in 1883, Milford House began catering to tourists, primarily American sportsmen, as many as 100 at a time and 700 in a single season, by the early 1900s. Business was so brisk the original house was enlarged on four occasions with overflow guests boarding in neighbouring private homes. There are said to be 50 lakes within 10 miles of Milford House, a drawing card for the avid angler and canoeist.

Local guides like Louis Harlow (working a peavey atop logs at right) constructed 25 log cabins at Milford House along the shores of Geier and Boot lakes. Del Thomas is standing in the centre. Although the first two cabins were finished in 1902, the majority were built during the 1920s.

A postcard of "cabin row" at Milford House, c.1920. Many were privately owned. Del Thomas would lease a parcel of land for a dollar a year on the condition that control reverted to Milford House on the cabin owner's death. A shrewd businessman, Thomas insisted all meals be taken in the hotel dining room. Cabins were still using an inside privy and oil lamps in the 1960s.

Milford House provided two "rustic" camps at Eleven Mile Lake for hunting and fishing parties – a cookhouse and sleeping cabin.

The Eleven Mile Lake cabins were used predominately for autumn moose hunting while fishing parties, which quite often involved families as shown here, tented during warmer months with trips lasting from two days to two weeks.

There was something for all ages at Milford House whether it be netting a trout, landing a kiss or enjoying a reflective moment on the cabin porch (top right, facing page).

Milford House was popular with retired American military officers. One of the best known was Brigadier General Chambers McKibbin, 1841-1913 (above), who fought in the American Civil War and Spanish-American War. He was noted for his caustic tongue, displaying an "ability to damn everything in sight." Another officer of note was Colonel Eaton Albert Edwards (1845-1916), who died at Milford House July 16, 1916, of a heart attack while walking in the woods. Somber Milford guests later gathered at the tree where Edwards expired to erect a plaque (below). Both men are buried in Arlington National Cemetery in Washington, D.C.

"Monster" picnics at McKibbin's Beach were popular summer activities, with Milford guides in charge of cooking corned beef hash and pancakes. On one occasion 200 lobsters were boiled up, having been purchased for $6 from fishermen at Parker's Cove on the Bay of Fundy shore near Annapolis Royal.

"Whatever may be your scruples against the use of liquors, don't go into the woods without whisky – rye or Scotch, according to preference. Alcohol, of course, is good for poison ivy, but whisky is better. Maybe it is because of the drugs that wicked men are said to put into it. ... It is well to carry one's morals into the woods, but if I had to leave either behind, I should take the whisky." – Albert Bigelow Paine

Enjoying cake and iced tea perhaps. Or are these Milfordites imbibing a stronger beverage?

It was common for at least 15 or 20 young people to be staying at Milford House during the summer. For many years, Jamie Kilbourne, a former Broadway dancer, assumed the role of volunteer activities director, organizing music recitals, barbershop quartets, plays, kazoo ensembles (above) and costume parties (below). Guests pooled their resources to build a large hall they called the Casino, where nightly dances were held with accompaniment provided by piano and gramophone records.

There were numerous outdoor activities including Indian and settler days, as depicted here, tennis and croquet matches (rumoured to be "no game for sissies"), spirited renditions of capture the flag between teams of "rumrunners" and "coast guards" using empty liquor bottles, and baseball games pitting Rumhounds against the Neversweats (rum, it would seem, was popular at Milford House). Baseball games were said to be lighthearted contests for all ages, incorporating "a lot of horseplay," an old tennis ball pitched underhand, no called balls or strikes, and adults batting one-handed.

Boathouse.

The Milford House lakes – Geier and Boot – were the hub of many water activities including canoeing, rowing, swimming, log rolling, even model yacht regattas with guests entering elaborate handmade miniature sailing vessels.

Judges/viewing tower.

Note the attire worn for a leisurely paddle along the shoreline or an expeditionary foray down the lake, complete with dress shirt and tie.

No details could be found to identify the festive occasion for which this flotilla of canoes was decorated. In the bottom photo on the left, Milford House's most famous guest, Eddie Breck, displayed a naval theme with his entry, the NL possibly standing for Navy League.

Dr. Edward (Eddie) Breck (1861-1929) (opposite)

Eddie Breck was born in San Francisco. His father, Joseph Breck, a captain in the United States Navy, died in 1865 of pneumonia. Eddie's mother, Ellen Francis Newell Breck, was an "adventuresome lady" from a "proper Boston family," who sailed with her husband in the Orient and gave birth to son Jack "somewhere off Guam." Following Joseph's death, she married a wealthy Bostonian by the name of Rice. When he too died young, Ellen never remarried, choosing instead to dedicate her life to raising two sons who attended the best of schools. Eddie was educated at Oberlin and Amherst colleges and Cambridge, Munich and Leipzig universities, receiving his PhD in 1887. He trained in voice and theatre while living in Europe and was considered a "talented" violinist. Eddie taught at Amherst College for many years.

Eddie Breck was considered to be charismatic as well as egotistical ("not conspicuously modest," as one person put it). "Somehow [Breck] exacted from everybody the homage of calling him DOCTOR. You could almost hear the capitals." He once asked another doctor, "Are you a real doctor or just a saw-bones?"

In 1889, Eddie, shown here in costume during his drama days in Germany, married "a petite lady with a big name," Antonia (Toni) Victorina Wagner Von Kleeblatt (right), an Austrian soprano opera singer who went by the stage name of Madame Beaumont.

Joseph Breck, Eddie's father, was a Lieutenant Commander in the Union Navy during the American Civil War. For his exemplary military service blockading the Confederate South, the United States government named a warship in his honour following World War I. The U.S.S. *Breck* brought Charles Lindbergh home in 1927 following his historic solo flight across the Atlantic Ocean.

Eddie's brother, John (Jack) Leslie Breck, 1860-1899, trained as an artist at the Royal Art Academy in Leipzig. By the late 1880s, Jack was considered a "prominent pioneering American Impressionist" in France, having painted with Claude Monet while supposedly engaging in a romantic tryst with Monet's stepdaughter Blanche. Jack is credited with introducing the Impressionist painting style to Boston in 1890 with a solo exhibition at the St. Botolph Club.

Lieutenant Commander Edward Breck retired in 1925 at the age of 64 from U.S. Naval Intelligence. In recognition of an illustrious military career, he received the Navy Cross "for distinguished and dangerous service," was made a Chevalier of the Legion of Honor (France), a Commander of the Order of Aviz (Portugal), and was awarded the Order of Christ and D.S.M. (Portugal). Breck served as curator of Naval Archives in Washington D.C. and was a member of the Loyal Legion, the Order of Foreign Wars, the Society of Colonial Wars, the Army and Navy Club, the American Historical Association, and the U.S. Naval Institute.

Eddie Breck, his wife Toni, and daughters Josephine (left), Margaret (Peggy) (right), Nellie (seated). Eddie is said to have enjoyed "public limelight" but had little interest in "domestic matters." Breck's daughters attended Edgehill girls' school in Windsor, Nova Scotia, some winters while he pursued his world adventures. He eventually divorced Toni and married Mary Louise Stanley, in 1923, who continued to come to Milford House in the 1930s after his death.

Ellen Francis (Nellie) Breck, born in Prague in 1890, was the oldest of the three Breck children and said to be Eddie's favourite because she enjoyed tramping the woods as much as her father did.

Eddie Breck owned two cabins at Milford House, one named Buckshaw where he resided and a second building near the shore of Boot Lake called Doeshaw which served as his writing retreat.

Sunday was poker day at Breck's cabin with a select group of guides and guests gathered for drinks poured by young Farish Owen (below, right), who first went to Milford House in 1902 at eight years of age. His reminisces appear in *Guides of the North Woods*.

It's not known when Eddie Breck first arrived at Milford House or what attracted him. Being from Boston, he possibly came as early as the 1880s, drawn by the writings of a Mr. Woodman, an American sportsman who fished the Milford Lakes and published a glowing account of his visit in the Boston newspapers. Thanks to Breck's propensity for taking photographs – in two of these shots he's holding a camera – we have a wonderful record of his Milford House days that were discovered in old family albums.

Eddie Breck edited a 136-page tourism booklet for the Maritime Board of Trade in 1909 entitled *Sporting Guide to Nova Scotia* (opposite). The photos on these two pages provide a collage showing some of his experiences in the Milford woods. Note the eating tray fashioned from a moose antler in the bottom left photo.

Eddie Breck wrote many articles c.1909-1914 for newspapers and sporting magazines, including *Outing* and *Forest & Stream*. He covered a wide range of topics, such as trout fishing, caribou hunting in Cape Breton, moose calling, still-hunting, snowshoeing, whitewater canoeing, game laws, conservation, guides and guide meets.

"Hunting the Wildcat" by Eddie Breck appeared in the March 1912 issue of *Outing* magazine. Included with the article, which focused on Charlie Charleton, was this picture (bottom) featuring Charlie (middle) and his photogenic hound Jack in the winter woods of Annapolis County.

Eddie Breck took this picture which he used in a 1911 article for *Outing* magazine entitled "Still-hunting Moose in 'Calling' Time." All that is known about the woodsman featured here is what Eddie tells us. "A city-feller who loves the woods, known to his intimates as Unk [a name that often turns up in Breck's writings], a mighty man of science with ideas of his own ... Unk was fairly normal, though he had an expensive predilection for cornbeef hash; expensive, I mean, in weight, for not alone are tinned cubes of cornbeef heavy, but the potatoes that go with the beef are nearly as heavy and bulky."

Eddie Breck (seated at right, above, and kneeling, below) published a 430-page tome in 1908, *The Way of the Woods: A Manual for Sportsmen in Northeastern United States and Canada*. The book sold for $1.75. Glowing reviews no doubt stroked an already inflated ego: "The Encyclopedia Britannica of the woods" (*Independent*); "It is amazing that one man should know so much and be able to tell it so well." (*Philadelphia Inquirer*); "The best handbook for woodsmen we have ever seen." (*Boston Advertiser*).

Eddie Breck included this photo of his daughter Nellie in the chapter "Women in the Woods."

There are 22 chapters in *The Way of the Woods* covering an array of topics such as clothing, canoes, provisions, cookery, making camp, hunting, fishing, nature protection, photography, hygiene, medicine and surgery. One four-page dissertation about "Women in the Woods" is included here in its entirety.

"The average woman of 1830 had a traditional dread of everything mannish; she cultivated the languid; her appetite was rather delicate; she was given to fainting. If she could have foreseen the Yankee girl of 1908 she would have believed that the Amazons had returned to life and emigrated from the banks of the Thermodon to people the United States. And of a truth the girl of the day is a different being from her grandmother, taller, stronger, healthier. All she has lost is just a bit of womanly tenderness, after all a real loss, but more than compensated for by her gains. She has been benefited even more than her brother by the 'nearer to nature' movement, and sports have become almost as much a part of her life as of his. There is no reason why she should not imitate her ancestress who accompanied her husband into the wilderness and there carved out a home.

The only woman identified is Nellie Breck, on the right.

"Camping-out may be made as easy as one likes, and her participation in the more strenuous phases of forest life, as big game hunting, or mountaineering, may depend alone on her physical prowess. One other thing, however, she will probably do well to consider, namely, the question whether or not she is really wanted on the trip; for there is unfortunately a very large class of male sportsman who absolutely refuse to be 'bothered by womenfolks in camp.' It must be confessed that in too many cases a man takes his ladies into the woods entirely on their account, from a sense of duty, and that ladies in the majority of cases are really a bother, for they require, tacitly if not actually, constant attention of one kind or the other, and their comparative lack of mobility hampers the movements of the party. I say 'in the majority of cases,' for women there are who fall in with forest ways so readily, and who help themselves, and understand how to make the men feel at liberty to do what they like without regard to them (all in reason of course), to the extent that the lords of creation at the end of the trip vote them 'bricks' and 'not a bit in the way.' That in high praise for the woman camper, which she should strive to merit.

"Several women with experience in camping have favoured me with their views, and the gist of their wisdom. It is understood that spring and summer are the seasons in question.

Outer Dress: Full duxbak or khaki suit with fairly short skirt: extra cloth skirt; brown or dark knickerbockers. Silk neckerchief. Canvas leggings.

Underwear: Two or three sets, medium weight combination flannels.

Shirts: Grey flannel shirt, similar to men's, with watch-pocket in breast. Sweater.

Stockings: 3 or 4 pair coarse cotton (or silk or light wool?) for high boots. Heavy wool stockings for moccasins.

Headgear: Felt hat with stiff brim (to keep veil from face) or straw sailor-hat. Dark chiffon veil. Black silk head-net.

Gloves: Pair of thick chamois. Rubber gloves if much washing or other camp-work is to be done.

Footwear: High waterproof lace-boots for tramping. Moccasins for canoe. Felt slippers for camp. Knit bed-socks.

Toilet-articles: Tooth-brush, tooth-powder, hand-mirror, brush and comb, soap in celluloid case, leather bottle-case, sponge-bag.

Medicines, etc: In bottle-case: Pond's Extract, brandy, Jamaica ginger, vial ammonia, soda-mint tablets, cold-cream.

Specialities: Rubber wash-basin. Two small nesting pails for hot and cold water. (Here the author raises his eyebrows!)

Waterproofs, etc: Yachting oilskin jacket. Light-weight rubber poncho. Rubber hood with cape.

Charlie Charleton and a bug-netted lady sport pause for the camera.

Del Thomas helps Nellie Breck (left) and her sister Peggy move a box of clothing, possibly to their cabin as Nellie is carrying an oil lamp.

Front row, left to right: guide ?, Nellie Breck, guide ?, possibly second wife Mary, and Eddie Breck. Back row left to right: guide ?, guide ?, Louis Harlow, and Charlie Charleton.

"The important thing to cultivate is independence. Let the men of the party once discover that the lady does not require to be mollicoddled or waited on all day long and that she is a 'good sport,' which is another way of saying that she takes everything as it comes, and her path will be easy, as well as that of her male companions. But from the nervous woman, or the petulant one, or her who screams at sight of a mouse or an innocent daddy-longlegs – good Lord deliver us! It is mostly a matter of that first of social qualities, tact. Blessed is she who is helpful without seeming to interfere; happy is she who is not afraid that her hands will roughen, her feet grow broad, and her crow's-feet deepen.

"A word in regard to appearance. Men like women to be real women, to be modest, and to be as good-looking as they can be. Modesty is not so much a matter of dress as of demeanour. One woman can wear knickerbockers without a skirt and appear perfectly natural and modest while another simply can't. But, in the name of all that is beautiful and practical, do not wear those things called bloomers, great formless baggy balloons, that are as ugly as they are awkward. Knickers should be well-fitting though loose and easy and should be gathered below the knee either by straps or light elastics."

Eddie Breck, far right, with family members and guides.

Left to right: ?; ?; ?; Nellie Breck holding an axe over her shoulder; possibly her husband Forrest MacNee; Nellie's mother Toni Breck seated by the fire, ?; ?. Many people in the photos in the family albums were not identified.

It appears Eddie Breck was not pleased with his portrayal in *The Tent Dwellers*. In the March 1, 1913, edition of *Forest & Stream* he wrote a humorous rebuttal; a portion is repeated here.

"A great painter of the Renaissance once got even with a bitter enemy, whose political position rendered him otherwise immune, by immortalizing him in a celebrated painting of the Inferno as one of the principal devils. The method always appealed to me, and I have a list of certain individuals whose characters I have long contemplated placing in a very lurid literary Inferno. Judge, then, of my indignant astonishment when, before I had gathered sufficient courage for the attack, to find this method tried on myself!

"You have all read this calumnious caricature of a pure and simple soul offered to a jeering public under the title of *The Tent Dwellers* which purports to relate the adventures of the author, two Bluenose guides and my very humble self.

"Now this man came down to my cabin in the woods with a halo of innocence about his head and begged forsooth for the privilege of enjoying the primitive wilderness in my experienced company, etc. And in the largeness of my heart I took him in, this viper, and warmed him for weeks in my bosom. I opened to him the wondrous secrets of the great unknown. For days and days we paddled and fished and slept shoulder to shoulder while he covertly studied me at this close range, he and his insidious camera. Worse yet, he entered into a foul conspiracy with a man who heaves charcoal for the magazines, to issue caricatures of me, a respectable, habitually good-looking person, in the public press.

"You know the deplorable result, the book has sold like wildfire, and the length of two normal lives would not suffice me to eliminate those staring goggles and that dervish beard from literature. Two considerations particularly irritated me; firstly, that not one cent of the big royalties on this book ever dropped into my yawning coffers, directly, anyhow; and, secondly, that the artist not only handed down to posterity a totally wrong impression of my particular style of beauty, but actually had the appalling assurance to make that man Allie [Albert Bigelow Paine], really a shambling, over-grown creature, go down in history as an Adonis.

The "begoggled" Eddie Breck with "dervish beard" as sketched by Hy Watson for *The Tent Dwellers*.

"When the book first appeared, I thought only of blood. The double murder of a prominent author and a well-known artist, followed by a sensational homicide, in self-defense, would not only assuage my thirst for vengeance, but drag me out of the semi-nirvana in which an apathetic public had thus far left me to languish. But something – was it my New England conscience? – caused me to abandon this fell plan, and I determined to sue both author and artist for defamation of character. But again it occurred to me that such a *cause celebre* would only tend to increase the sale of the book, and thus put more money into my enemies' purses. Also I should be laughed at for not possessing timber heroic enough to take a joke, even when it resulted in my being placed on record for all time as a begoggled and hirsute anarchist..." [*The Tent Dwellers* and Breck's book *The Way of the Woods* were published the same year, 1908.]

Eddie Breck was an avid hunter when he first came to Milford House, as shown by these photos taken at his cabin. Note the deer heads flanking the cabin door in the photo below. But the passion waned in later years when he became a proponent of studying wildlife and shooting it with a camera rather than a rifle. He also campaigned vigorously against the use of leghold traps to catch fur-bearing animals.

Eddie Breck published a second book, *Wilderness Pets at Camp Buckshaw* in 1910, about the various animals he studied and raised while living in his cabin at Milford House.

Camp Buckshaw was home to all manner of creatures including deer, loons, bullfrogs, beavers; two porcupines named Pompey and Julius Caesar; a crow, Jim, which "did not prove to be a particularly brilliant specimen of his race"; two ravens, Lige and Elijah; three seagulls – Tim, Giroflé and Girofla, the latter two named for an opera; and a house cat Yankee.

This photo of a non-indigenous bear is somewhat of a mystery. As the backdrop is unquestionably Milford House and the handlers and equipment indicate something more than a Camp Buckshaw pet, it could be a travelling circus passing through.

Yankee the cat is playfully reaching out to Pompey the porcupine, which may or may not have been a wise thing to do.

At left, the ravens Lige and Elijah and on the right is Eddie Breck and Jim the crow.

Breck with two seagulls, at left. Inquiring minds want to know if Yankee is posing with a laid-back or deceased wild cousin on the right. Eddie's gloves could indicate the critter was in the here and now, or that it was a coolish day. Both cats are fixated on something to Breck's left, but Yankee appears alert while Bob is somewhat spaced out, indicating he's been medicated or …

Black bear cubs Sukey, Connie and Rube. Two of the imps got loose one day in Eddie Breck's cabin and ransacked the place, spreading molasses and booze throughout. Not everyone at Milford House shared Eddie's enthusiasm for his menagerie of wild pets.

One of the cubs enjoys a snort while Jim the crow looks on. For the winter months the bruins were sent south "to a certain zoological garden in New England."

Possibly Eddie Breck's prized calf moose Nigghy.

Albert Bigelow Paine wrote in *The Tent Dwellers* that as they paddled the Shelburne River near Irving Lake, Charlie Charleton and Del Thomas became "absorbed in the possibility" of spotting moose. "Such is the passion for this animal among Nova Scotia guides, that whatever the season or the purpose of the expedition, and however triumphant its result, it is accounted a disappointment and a failure by the natives when it ends without at least a glimpse of a moose. … I discovered presently that [Eddie] was ambitious to send a specimen of a moose calf, dead or alive, to the British Museum, and would improve any opportunity to acquire that asset.

"I may say that I was opposed to any such purpose. I am overfond of Eddie, and I wanted him to have a good standing with the museum people, but I did not like the idea of slaughtering a little calf moose before its mother's very eyes, and I did not approve of its capture, either. Even if the mother moose could be convinced that our intentions were good, and was willing to have her offspring civilized and in the British Museum, or Zoo, or some other distinguished place, I still opposed the general scheme.

"It did not seem to me that a calf moose tied either outside or inside of our tent for a period of weeks, to bleat and tear around, and to kick over and muss up things generally, would be a proper feature to add to a well-ordered camp, especially if it kept raining and we had to bring him inside. I knew that eventually he would own the tent, and probably demand a sleeping bag. I knew that I should have to give him mine, or at least share it with him."

Nigghy was short for Nigghiajootch, meaning "little moose" in Mi'kmaq. The woman in the head net has been identified by some as Mary Breck, Eddie's second wife. If correct, this is a different moose as Eddie wrote of Nigghy in 1910, years before he divorced Toni.

Paine did not write in jest that Eddie Breck was "ambitious to send a specimen of a moose calf, dead or alive, to the British Museum." Breck tells in *Wilderness Pets of Camp Buckshaw* that he "had been commissioned by a great museum to capture for its collection a new-born calf-moose … and that a big envelope had come from Halifax containing the authority to make the capture."

The actual "capture" didn't take place until a year or two following *The Tent Dwellers* expedition and was successfully carried out in closer proximity to Milford House by Mi'kmaq guide Sam Glode. Breck wrote that "Niggy's fame quite outshone that of the other pets, and people flocked in from miles round Milford to see him."

Sadly the story does not end well for Nigghy, as he died unexpectedly at Milford House as a result of falling into a hole while being pursued by a hound. "Poor little Nigghy! And so the Museum got him after all," lamented Breck. "He was the dearest, gentlest, most confiding little pet that ever lived. Ned Buckshaw [Breck's pseudonym] reproached himself bitterly for taking Nigghy at all, for not protecting him more carefully, and for everything else connected with his short career."

Eddie and daughter Nellie enjoy a quiet moment on the lake shore. Nellie, a trained nurse, was only 40 years of age when she died in 1930.

Dr. Edward Breck died of a heart attack at Milford House on May 14, 1929, and was buried in Arlington National Cemetery, Washington, D.C. The loss of Eddie Breck to the Elite Sport Tourist Era was as significant an event in the history of Nova Scotia tourism as Campbell Hardy's return to England during the Military Tourist Era.

Grampy Eddie and possibly Allen MacNee, Nellie's son.

Chapter 2
Long Pull To The Shelburne
by M.B. Miller 1911

Francis Parkman [Jr., 1823-1893] in that charming work *Pioneers of France in the New World* [Little, Brown & Co, 1865], tells in inimitable style how DeMonts on his first voyage to America, in 1604, armed with letters-patent granting him enormous lands and privileges south of the St. Lawrence, captured and made prize of a fur trading ship and cargo and consoled its commander by bestowing his name upon the scene of his misfortune. This highhanded poacher, one Rossignol, was a fellow countryman of DeMonts, and the scene of his discomfiture is now known as Liverpool Harbour, but his name still lives in connection with the largest lake in Nova Scotia.

Lake Rossignol is about eighteen miles long and in many places six or seven miles wide. Its outline is irregular and toward the northern and southern ends is varied by numerous bays and coves. Halfway down on the eastern shore is Second Lake and just beyond it First Lake, but both clearly a part of the main lake, while at the southern end are Fourth and Fifth lakes, similarly placed. Off in the woods to the north, east and south are many scattered groups of smaller lakes all draining into Rossignol, and to the west is the Shelburne River. The outlet is at the lower end of First Lake, where the great torrent of water pours out to form the Mersey. Here are the famous Indian Gardens, a fine parklike point of land between the lake and river which, in ancient times, was a favorite meeting place of the aboriginal Micmacs and now is popular with the white men for the big trout which abound in the heavy water.

In the face of a fresh south wind we went down the lake toward Wildcat Point. We might have anticipated what was coming, as we had had perfect days since leaving home and a change was probably due; besides the guides had consulted the new moon and reported it wet, but to us, from the States, a wind from the south could not possibly mean bad weather. Alas! we were to learn that in Nova Scotia the storms were perfectly impartial when it came to the points of the compass. However, we gave no concern for the morrow as we made camp at the furthermost end of the point, with a level place for the tents, good shelter and plenty of wood.

Milford guide Charlie Charleton (left) whiles away some time playing cards. Skat, the game of choice on Miller's trip, originated c.1810-1817 as a three-player game using a deck of 32 cards.

Lawrence pitched the tents facing each other, with the fire between them, and in selecting just the right angle to allow the warmth of the fire to penetrate the tents and at the same time to permit the smoke to blow away, he showed a remarkable prescience of the wind and weather we were to have for the next three days. In the meantime, Horace and Charles, as cooks, prepared a delicious trout chowder, and also served boiled rice and raisins sweetened with maple syrup. In the evening George gave a lesson in skat to two unpromising pupils.

We all slept well and did not stir until half past five. The clouds hung low and threateningly, and the south wind had freshened. Altogether it looked dubious about venturing out on the lake for the long pull to the Shelburne. Our sixteen-foot Fredericton canoes were steady, seaworthy little boats, but they were heavily loaded and a canoe after all is only a canoe. But we did not give up without a struggle.

A fishing party from Bear River – guide Dube Rice (facing camera), sport Dr. Guy Victor Turnbull (left), May Turnbull, and guide Les Rice – takes a break at Long Garden Carry, Digby County, 1928, to enjoy a game of cards. Cribbage and 45s have been a mainstay in the Nova Scotia woods.

An unidentified woodsman, possibly a Milford House Guide, shows off a speckled beauty.

After breakfast the three guides took one of the canoes, and after getting aboard at the little sheltered cove swung out to the windward side of the point to try the seas while we watched them from the shore. They were very thoroughly shaken up by the rough seas. We decided not to attempt a venture which might result disastrously.

To occupy the day it was agreed that we should cross the sheltered bay to the lee of Wildcat Point and retrace some of the distance up the Keejeemacoojee, fishing as we went. This we did and had fair results, considering that it soon commenced to rain and the wind kept growing stronger, so that in many places it was difficult to cast. We caught fifty-four trout. Gurney was high rod, but the Scribe took home the flag with a fine fish $16\frac{1}{2}$ inches long, easily topping in weight Gurney's big trout of the day before.

We lunched in the rain on beans, cold tongue, tea and marmalade, but were not dismayed by the steady downpour, as three very new, very complete and very yellow oilskins were the most conspicuous feature of the landscape. We met three parties in boats on the river, which surprised us until we recalled that it was the 24th of May, the day on which, according to schedule, we were not to be crowded at Indian Gardens. We saw several ducks, two loons out on the lake, and a porcupine chewing away at the bark of a maple.

A guide's culinary skills could be severely tested on a month-long canoe trip with trout, shown here in the pan, being the staple food for three meals a day.

In returning to camp the increased wind had so decidedly stirred up the lake that it was apparently risky to attempt the straight run to Wildcat Point, so we followed somewhat the shores of the intervening bay. We did not all go that way quite as directly as we might. George and Gurney with their guides had gotten a start for home and Lawrence with the Scribe were following on some distance behind. Lawrence saw the two canoes ahead turn circuitously to avoid the full force of the wind and waves, but he decided to take his canoe straight across to save time. The Scribe didn't say anything but started thinking, and presently mental telepathy got in its work and Lawrence concluded that after all the long way round might be better.

When we got back, a brisk fire soon dried and thawed us out. Supper afforded us the novelty of baked trout, which might have tasted better if we had not been led up to it past ample quantities of trout chowder and fried trout. The guides, however, never lost their appetites for trout, and Lawrence and Horace had an exciting trout eating contest that night. Lawrence won, hands down, with a score of five and a half to two. Five and half trout of the size we were catching merits a championship. That night the wind was very fresh from the southwest, and a steady rain was falling, but we were filled with a good supper, and with a blazing big fire in front of the tents were able to accept the situation philosophically.

"For about an hour we had fine sport. George took eight and the scribe nine splendid trout."

The next day started early for some of us. As Gurney was anxious about an expected telegram, which had not arrived before we left Milford, he had decided the night before, in view of the probable continuance of the storm, to spend the day in going out to Caledonia where he could reach Mr. Thomas over the telephone. He and Lawrence were up at 3 o'clock and an hour later paddled two miles to Lowe's Landing, where they secured a horse and wagon, so that Gurney was able to drive the thirteen miles to Caledonia, accomplish his mission, and get back to camp by mid-afternoon.

In the meantime Horace and Charles, after a careful survey, determined to take some of the heavier dunnage, and attempt to reach the Shelburne. This they did successfully, but in coming back they had a hard, anxious time, as the lake was running full of seas like the ocean.

After lunch we two, with the guides, took the canoes and paddling in the lee of the shore worked our way around once more to the Keejeemacoojee. For about an hour we had fine sport. George took eight and the scribe nine splendid trout. All of the latter's were over eleven inches long, a pound and a quarter and a pound and an eighth being the largest, but George that day proved himself the best fisherman on the trip by catching, after an exciting, gruelling contest, a beautifully proportioned and colored trout which just tipped the scales at a pound and three-quarters. He also hooked and landed a double of two pounds and a quarter of hard fighting energy on a light rod and tackle. We brought in nine fish all over a foot long – great, beautiful, lusty wild trout.

American Philip Hooper Moore (1879-1961) wore many hats – professional engineer; ardent sportsman; CBC Halifax radio personality who went by the pseudonym Joe Kose, the Nova Scotia guide; contributor to hunting and fishing magazines including *Outdoor Life* and *Field & Stream*; published author (*Castle Buck*; *Rossignol Rhymes*); and promoter of early Nova Scotia guide meets and U.S.-based sportsmen shows. Phil Moore lost his Lake Rossignol camp to flooding in 1928 when a dam was built on the Mersey River at Indian Gardens to generate electricity for a Bowater Mersey Paper Co. pulp mill 20 miles downstream at Brooklyn, Queens County. The ensuing rise in water levels merged 10 smaller lakes into one, turning Lake Rossignol, already Nova Scotia's largest freshwater lake, into a behemoth.

When we got back Gurney and Lawrence were home and entertaining two visitors, P[hilip] H. Moore of New York, who had just opened a new camp for sportsmen, and his head guide, Joe Patterson. Their camp, Camp Rossignol, is at Lowe's Landing, and they came across to call on us in a motorboat. We were glad to see them, but shuddered a little at the thought of a motorboat in that beautiful wilderness, and wondered how long it would be before the loons on the lake would move away.

After they were gone we admiringly inspected Gurney's purchases in Caledonia, smoking tobacco and chocolate and six dozen eggs. We had twelve dozen of the latter already, but Gurney, as one of the greatest living egg eaters, had thought we might run short, and with a sublime devotion – to whom or what I shall not say – had carried through the driving rain and over thirteen miles of road, a large part of which was corduroy, those six dozen eggs on his lap.

White Point Beach Lodge, c.1930. When Phil Moore was forced out of Camp Rossignol at Lowe's Landing in 1928, he built new hunting and fishing camps at Indian Gardens and Broad River Lake. In addition, he opened White Point Beach Lodge (a.k.a. Moore's Camp) near Liverpool, Queens County, which featured cabins and an eight-room resort with a dining room (all buildings were constructed of split logs), a 9-hole golf course and tennis courts. Unfortunately for Moore, he went bankrupt after a couple of years, a casualty of the Great Depression perhaps. White Point went into receivership, but was soon resurrected. The saltwater retreat catered heavily to tuna fishermen, as interest in that sport mushroomed into an international fishing event during the mid-1930s. White Point Beach Resort is still operational today.

Next morning there was no change in the atmospheric conditions. That interminable storm continued to blow and to create a watery tumult on the lake which entirely precluded successful canoeing. Our clothing and blankets were commencing to get damp and there were times when even the hardiest member of the party admitted that he was cold. Besides the sending down to the Shelburne of the heavy provisions had limited the variety of the menu. But matters might have been worse. Later we paddled once more to the Keejeemacoojee River, our only place of diversion. In contrast to the day before we only had indifferent luck, with few fish and those mostly small, but we added twenty-nine more to the record.

On a pretty, mossy bank under some evergreens we lunched on baked beans and tea, and shortly afterward, deceived by the less boisterous wind on the sheltered river, we hurried back to camp in the hopes of improved weather conditions. On the contrary we found things a shade worse. The wind had shifted back from the southwest to the south, it was high, and squalls of rain kept chasing each other across the lake.

Bear hunter Henry Day (shown here) from Salmon River, Halifax County, killed 100 bruins in his day. David Trueman Costley dispatched 300 in Kings and Lunenburg counties, earning him the title of World Champion Bear Killer (see *Guides of the North Woods* for his story). Unfortunately, no biographical material or printable photographs of Pat Lacey could be found, although Eddie Breck did write of him in an article for *Outing* magazine.

On our return we found in camp an old trapper and his boy who were on their way to visit some bear traps off to the westward. They had a rowboat, but not much else, so it did not require a great deal of urging to persuade them to stay over night with us. Pat Lacey was his name; he travels winter and summer alike with a repeater, and his chief dividend payers are bears, wildcats, foxes, otter, mink and muskrats.

The morning of the 27th, George awakened the camp by the loud announcement, "Get up, boys, the storm is over." This was about 4:30, and I have no hesitancy in saying that if, by any chance, there had been a mistake in his estimate of the weather, something serious might have overtaken him then and there. As it was we had gotten so thoroughly weary of Wildcat Point that we turned out most amiably, and after a look around, hopes grew high that at last we could get on to the Shelburne River. The wind had changed from gusts and squalls to a pleasant steady breeze, and there was a different quality to the air.

By 6 o'clock we were ready to start. Pat Lacey, who was traveling light with only a rifle, an axe and a tiny kit, kindly took into his capacious rowboat some of our heavier things and started on ahead, but even then the canoes had quite load enough to carry into the turbulent seas still remaining from the storm. This first part of the six-mile run to the mouth of the Shelburne was by all odds the roughest, as before long we commenced to avail ourselves of quieter water in the lee of some of the pretty islands which stud the western end of the lake. As we paddled steadily on, the clouds grew lighter and an occasional patch of blue sky gave promise of a fine day. In this we were not disappointed.

When approximately two-thirds of the distance had been covered, the ever alert Lawrence called out, "See the moose!" And again a moment later, "There's a calf with her."

We were three or four hundred yards from a small island when we saw a cow moose in the water just beyond it swimming toward another island at right angles to our course. A few feet behind her was the calf. The cow at first swam quite slowly, swaying her big mule-like head from side to side most awkwardly. We paddled hard to head her off, anxious to stop the calf, as he was such a little chap that we feared he might drown in the effort to follow his mother. She kept on at a quickened rate, but Gurney and Horace, by making their canoe fairly fly through the water, managed to get quite close as she went ashore at the further island, and Gurney was able to photograph her. Their canoe was then swung around to the other side of the island to round her up and to prevent her, if possible, from keeping straight on across the lake.

In the meantime the calf had turned back, and when the rest of us came up he was standing in the water on the rocks, a pitiful little object of misery, now and then blatting out his loneliness as only a moose calf can. Apparently he was not much frightened by us, but was well blown by his swim. We sat in the canoes scarcely a dozen feet away and could easily have captured him if we had wished, but we did not want to put the man smell on him, or do anything which might make his already greatly disturbed mother permanently desert him. Gurney and Horace finally succeeded in turning her back, and when we last saw her, as we paddled on down the lake, she was swimming in a wide circle, but evidently working her way back to the young one. Later we learned from Pat Lacey, who was still keeping ahead of us, that he had seen both cow and calf swim to the island where we saw them, and it was a fair guess that he had first startled them out of cover.

Eddie Breck took these two pictures of a moose calf (possibly Nigghy) in the wild.

"No expedition in Nova Scotia is a success without having seen at least one moose." – Albert Bigelow Paine

"Swift water meant trout ..."

About this time in the spring the cow moose are apt to seek shelter on the islands in the lakes to have their young, thereby getting away from bears and wildcats, particularly the former, which are reputed to be very partial to calf moose. The young cows, as a rule, have one calf, the older ones almost invariably have two. Sometimes the latter ignore the island refuge and have their calves on the mainland, depending upon strength, prowess and maternal vigilance to fight off marauding bears. Someone, not as well versed in faunal lore as our guides, cited it as a wonderful example of the protection nature gives to her wild creatures that during this interesting period the cow moose had no scent, but the frank skepticism of our thoroughly moose-wise guides makes it necessary to record the statement as poetical, but probably not true.

Shelburne River was reached shortly before 8 o'clock. It is well to note before proceeding further that the Shelburne River bears no relation to the town on the south coast of similar name, as its waters flow into Lake Rossignol and thence into the Mersey. Shelburne town is on the Roseway close to its mouth at the head of Shelburne Harbor. Between the Mersey and the Roseway are the Sable and Jordan rivers, both sizeable streams. According to the guides it is an easy trip to go from Lake Rossignol to either the Jordan or the Roseway; the carries are not long or difficult and both rivers afford excellent fishing. The route to the Jordan is through the upper lakes connected directly with Rossignol; to the Roseway by way of the Little Tobeatic.

"The little river wound and turned amazingly and afforded us constantly changing vistas of sylvan beauty." A common scene in southwestern Nova Scotia depicting a placid water course meandering through a mix of woodland and barrens.

The Shelburne, our gateway to the upper country, was hard to locate on the lake shore until we were right upon its mouth. Here Pat Lacey went ashore with his boy to visit a long round of bear traps which he had out between the Shelburne and the Tobeatic lakes. A couple of hundred yards up stream brought us to rough water where the paddles were dropped and the spiked set poles taken up for the push through the falls. This was work which mainly fell upon the guides since the swift water meant trout, and we three could not resist the temptation to fish rather than to help; besides, the difficulties were not great and the pace was slow. Alternating with the falls, none very high or long, were stretches of stillwaters.

The little river wound and turned amazingly and afforded us constantly changing vistas of sylvan beauty. While we knew that the lumbermen had taken toll along this stream, we could see no evidence of it. The banks were richly clothed with trees of goodly size and beneath them the ground was carpeted with fresh green moss and ferns. About the middle of the morning we came to the first real carry of the trip, 300 yards, a little one which was to fade into insignificance in comparison with the mighty portages further along. This was at Kempton Dam. At another shallow runway, known as Pollard Falls, we saw the remains of an ancient log road, but further than these we noticed no evidences of human visitation.

We lunched on a large natural meadow gorgeously bespangled with the purple blooms of the "sheep kill," a member of the laurel family. A mile-long stillwater ran through it in broad, easy curves, dimpling in the gentle breeze. We boiled the kettle and ate our simple meal.

Near us at the water's edge a noisy specimen of the genus *Rana* attracted our attention by his boldness and reiterated vociferousness. One of us decided to try a little experiment, and taking his rod, swung a fly craftily in front of the pointed green nose. Quicker than the eye could follow, a soft tongue flew out and the fly disappeared, but almost as quickly came the strike, and froggy rose in the air, the most thoroughly astonished frog in Nova Scotia, to indulge in comical and wonderful acrobatics while the resilient rod held him dangling. In a moment he was released and the energy of the two or three jumps waterward, and the final dive gave us an inkling of his opinion of such feathered frauds as trout flies. It was a very funny episode, but perhaps there was an element of thoughtless cruelty about it.

However, it may be forgiven in the light of our general good behaviour since a less destructive party than ours never went into the woods. We had a very good pistol, but it was only used occasionally to demonstrate on a tin can target what utterly bad shots we were. At one time on the Sporting Lake stream, Gurney tried to shoot a swimming muskrat at an impossible distance, but nothing came of the attempt, and there were no others.

When it came to fishing, I may say while we took many trout every day, it was an invariable custom to return to the water unharmed all of them save a carefully estimated number which we kept to eat. We even went so far as to wet the hand before loosening the hook, so as to avoid the growth of fungus which sometimes attacks trout which have been roughly handled. The ones we kept were mercifully killed by breaking their necks.

"We boiled the kettle and ate our simple meal." Bear River guide Les Rice (left) and sport Guy Victor Turnbull from Digby enjoy lunch and a laugh at Johnnie McEwan's Carry, White Sand Stream, c.1930.

"About 4 o'clock we turned to the left and entered Sand Brook ... We went up it a short distance and camped in an open space ..."

We continued up the winding Shelburne, enjoying fully the warm bright day, watching the bird life, paddling through the stillwaters, and fishing the pools and rapids. The trout were not large, none weighing a pound, but we caught fifty-seven, and in the swift current even the medium-sized fish put up lively fights. We had those wretched little pests, the black flies, with us all day, but fortunately their attacks at no time were very serious or disturbing. About 4 o'clock we turned to the left and entered Sand Brook, a lovely little stream with clean white sand bottom. We went up it a short distance and camped in an open space amidst a grove of hemlocks, having made about twelve miles for the day. We needed the daylight hours remaining to dry the damp clothes, tents and blankets. Lawrence collected plenty of fragrant fir boughs for our beds, while Horace, threatened by the total exhaustion of the bread supply, with which we started, cooked biscuits in the reflecting oven.

During the manifold activities which occupied our attention before supper it was noticed that Gurney had become quiet and thoughtful. Presently, and with nothing to soften the shock, it came out – he was going in swimming! He would not presume to suggest that any one else in the party required more water than he had been getting right along, but for his part he did not mind confessing to friends that he needed a wash and proposed to get it. He had been looking at that brook with a calculating eye; it might be a bit shallow and the temperature of the water might leave something to be desired, but on the other hand it was clean, and the white sand bottom looked very attractive.

"I found to shave took off a good deal of valuable [fly] ointment each time." – Albert Bigelow Paine

The Scribe was so taken with Gurney's presentation of the matter that he said he would go in, too, but George, more cautious, was inclined to be conservative; said it would not give him the slightest trouble at all to sit on the bank and see that our clothes were not stolen; in fact, the more he thought about it the better he liked that job, and anyhow he had gotten his feet wet that day and he had long made it a rule of life never to go swimming with wet feet. He was hard to convince, but we finally got him.

My powers of description are utterly inadequate to draw the picture of the sequence of events which followed. I can only sketch in the barest outlines the scene on Sand Brook that sunny afternoon and leave to the imagination of the reader the filling in of details; how, in the process of undressing, each man kept a watchful eye on his neighbor that there might be no discourtesy in getting in first; how the black flies got in an inning which forced the situation; how Gurney waded in first and by a Spartan stoicism gave to us on the bank a false impression; how George and I finally mustered courage and got in up to our knees, the full depth of the stream; and how at this point I was so carried away by my feelings that George was unmercifully splashed by the commotion. I believe that Gurney really got all the way under, but George and I were perfectly satisfied with sundry dashes and splashes. Was that water really cold? Well, perchance if it had been iced it might have been a shade colder.

Sand Brook drains the Tobeatic Lakes. It had been our intention to make a detour at this place and to spend a couple of days in exploring the Big and Little Tobeatics, but after a conference we decided to omit this side trip, as we were apt to get better fishing elsewhere. However, after supper we three took Horace, and in one overloaded canoe paddled up the brook to the carry and then walked through the woods to take a look at Tupper Lake, the first of the Tobeatic group. We came out on a fine sand beach freshly marked with moose tracks, and before us stretched a beautiful sheet of water entirely surrounded by a primeval forest of pine and hemlock. Seen in the sunset light with the long shadows and the changing lights and shades, Tupper Lake was a gorgeously beautiful picture. On the way back we saw a porcupine high up in a hemlock tree, and heard an owl hooting somewhere in the hardwood.

We awoke after sleeping soundly on the fir boughs to find the sun had gotten the start on us. The guides told us that during the night there had been a little shower and later fine moonlight, but we had no regrets. One cannot be expected to see everything on a trip like this. Before us was another fine day with fresh, fair wind, blue sky and drifting clouds. We ran out on Sand Lake and one of the canoes went around the further side of an island in the hope of stirring out another cow moose, but nothing happened. A mile and a half of paddling took us through Sand Lake and then came a series of rough, rapid falls alternating with short stillwaters. At noon we had covered about five miles.

Practically everywhere we could catch trout, but they were of only ordinary size. This was a sore disappointment to Lawrence who had been extolling the size and game qualities of the Shelburne trout. He had assured us that the Shelburne waters held the grand-daddies of them all, but none of us could get past the pound mark. We even made Lawrence take a rod to see if some of the big fellows would recognize him, but alas without success. The few he landed only added to the poignancy of his grief.

Followed hard going. The stream was getting smaller and much shallower, the rapids succeeded each other almost without intervals, and it was necessary to permanently relieve the canoes of all weight possible. It was warm and the black flies surrounded each man like a halo. For hours the guides poled the canoes where the water was deep enough, wading and dragging them over the mossy rocks and sandy shallows. Gurney waded with the men, getting a few photographs of the stream, which scenically had no drawbacks, and now and then helping.

George and I followed a sort of trail through the woods, chiefly traveled by the peripatetic moose, and spent our energies in climbing waterfalls, crawling through thickets and waging war on the black flies. Evidently there were many moose in this section, as we were constantly coming upon fresh and old signs of them, and in several places we saw where they had yarded during the winter. We caught a few trout at favorable places where we could cast a fly, but the little black tormentors spoiled most of the pleasure of fishing. Finally we came out on Irwin Lake, another lovely stretch of water, sparkling in the western sunlight and looking most refreshing to our tired, hot party.

"It was warm and the black flies surrounded each man like a halo." Sport Willard Read fends off his tormentors with a towel while camped at Sixth Lake Carry, 1923.

"For hours the guides poled the canoes where the water was deep enough, wading and dragging them over the mossy rocks and sandy shallows."

This vintage picture from 1899 captured a thrashing trout being played toward a waiting dip net.

At the lower end of Irwin Lake there is an old loggers' dam. Close to the foot of the sloping logs, which form its backing, the rushing water forms two deep foam-covered pools. While the guides were making a short carry, Gurney had excellent fishing, while George and I watched admiringly his graceful and effective casting. He had taken two nice trout, each about a foot long, when suddenly a particularly vicious old brute struck with a tremendous swirl and carried away both flies and leader. The noise of the rushing water drowned his remarks, but we watched him lay on a new leader and flies and suspected that he was planning his revenge. Presently he started to work out along the sloping logs in order to reach just the right spot before trying a cast. But nothing further happened.

The paddle up Irwin Lake came as a pleasant rest after the laborious efforts which had preceded it. The wind was at our backs and the experimenting member of the party further lightened the work in his canoe by improvising a sail out of his khaki coat. This was the lake where Paine and Dell Thomas in *The Tent Dwellers* could not find the outlet, and, after vainly trying different coves, endeavored to go out the same way they had come in, until they discovered the current running the wrong way. We had no such trouble, nor was there much hard poling thereafter, as the stream ran more into stillwaters.

It was about a mile and a half across Irwin Lake, and at a similar distance above it we came to a stillwater brook which came into the main river from the right near the middle of an immense meadow. The banks of this brook were closely lined with cranberry bushes, the first we had seen. A third of a mile up it brought us to Lake Peblelugutch, rock-girdled and rock-studded, and a mile long. On the opposite shore was a hardwood ridge and we made our way to it at the north end of the lake to camp on the carry over into Pescawaw.

We had traveled about eleven miles since morning, and in direction northwest; had seen the first great blue heron of the trip, also a number of ducks, and just above Irwin Lake, Gurney photographed a particularly large porcupine. Last, but not least, we had caught seventy-six trout.

By this time we had become accustomed to the realities of camp life and had learned to create comfort and contentment out of the means at hand. The duties of the guides on making camp were well defined and the systematized efforts of each man directed along certain prearranged lines saved confusion and quickly accomplished results. At once upon reaching a proposed stopping place for the night the canoes were emptied and placed bottom up on shore, and immediately, without needless discussion or delay, each man turned to his allotted task.

Kedge guide Tom Canning cleans a trout – another of a guide's "defined" duties.

"The substantial fire required by the cook needed heavier wood and a hotter blaze. This was made of green hardwood logs ... placed in such a way across the stones as to secure a free draft."

Upon Charles devolved the duty of the fire, that most important factor in camp existence. In the absence of a fireplace already made for him by previous campers, he would lay two rows of stones a yard apart in front of the place selected for the tent. Then collecting some small dried sticks and a handful of leaves or birch bark, he would start a little blaze between the stones, usually by lighting some shavings, whittled off with his knife, and adding stick by stick the larger pieces until he had a presentable fire going. But the substantial fire required by the cook needed heavier wood and a hotter blaze. This was made of green hardwood logs, usually birch, and trees four or five inches thick were cut into five or six foot lengths and placed in such a way across the stones as to secure a free draft. It was curious to see how easily certain green hardwoods would burn in a going fire, and we learned that beech and maple burned equally as well as the birch.

In drenching wet weather it was sometimes hard to get the fire started, but the breaking up of an old stump usually supplied enough dry wood to get it going, and chief reliance would be placed on dead and dried logs, rather than on the green woods, to keep it up. For the night fire, which was supposed to keep the tents warm and to burn all night, Charles would get the largest dry log of pine or spruce that he and the others jointly were able to haul in, and with this for a back log and plenty of birch he would build up a fire which was not only comfortable, but also good to look upon.

"Our small wall tent afforded ample room for three to sleep in and had plenty of space overhead."

Lawrence had charge of the tents. The place selected depended solely upon the smoothness of the ground, and as the placing of the fire was subject to the location of the tent, it was promptly settled. Then the ground was gone over to remove all sticks and stones.

Our small wall tent afforded ample room for three to sleep in and had plenty of space overhead. In putting it up a stout forked sapling, nine or ten feet long, was cut, trimmed, pointed and driven firmly into the ground. Then a second upright was similarly driven at the proper distance in front for the other support of the ridge pole, or what was better, save in windy, rainy weather, two forked saplings, or now and then two of the set poles were lashed together and put up at angles of forty-five degrees. The purpose of this arrangement was to give an unobstructed entrance. The ridge pole was slipped under the peak of the tent, and it was raised and held taut by tying the guy ropes to a half dozen driven stakes two or three feet long. Over all came the fly, which was stretched over a pole laid on top of the ridge and drawn taut by means of separate longer stakes. It was further kept from contact with the roof in rainy weather by a couple of side poles on their own supports.

The guides were using a tent of curious model which only required one short upright and a few stakes. Its shape when up was not unlike half of a raised umbrella with the open side protected by flaps. Their tent was generally placed in front of us with the camp-fire between.

After the tents were up, if we camped near evergreens, Lawrence would start for a clump of them and presently return almost buried under a load of little green boughs strung on a limber withe. He always used the fir and not the spruce or hemlock, as the fir boughs were not prickly, lay smoothly, and had a delicious, woodsy smell. These little boughs he would imbricate from the back of the tent to the front, carefully sticking the broken end of each bough slantingly into the ground. Over the smooth, springy sweet-scented surface was stretched a piece of canvas the size of the floor of the tent, then individual ponchos, rubber side down, and finally the blankets. We each had two heavy black blankets of pure wool and weighing about eight pounds apiece. When on the move these were packed in a strong canvas bag which had straps for the shoulders.

The scheme in correctly making a bed was to fold two together on the long way, lay them on the ponchos and smooth out the wrinkles. The inside blanket was then overlapped for a foot of its edge and the outer one similarly tucked about the one within. The whole bed was then fixed by raising the excess at the foot and turning it up underneath until the remaining length corresponded approximately to the inches of the occupant. The unopened side of the two blankets was so placed that a man lying in his usual position had it to his back. In effect the result was that of a sleeping bag, and, like it, once in, it was not easy to get uncovered.

"The tent with its daily and nightly round becomes a rather important thing when it is to be a habitation for a period of weeks of sun and rain …" – Albert Bigelow Paine

The pillows were made up of our heavier clothing topped in the case of two of us by inflated air cushions, while the other used a small down pillow. The air pillows were not satisfactory, since before long leaks developed and rendered them worse than useless.

When it came to our personal sleeping habits, our ideas somewhat differed. George and Gurney doffed shoes, coats and hats, loosened buckles and buttons and turned in to sleep in their clothing, but I divested myself completely of my daytime garb, got into light flannel pajamas, and crawled into the blankets, perhaps to shiver and shake for a minute or two, but presently drift off into a dreamless slumber that could not be surpassed.

A square of canvas strung between some notched saplings often substituted for a tent.

It's quite probable Dr. Miller and his group unknowingly passed camps like the ones pictured on the next three pages, as locals would have used them for hunting, fishing, trapping and cutting timber. These two examples are c.1900 somewhere in Halifax County.

Kedge guides Art and Tom Canning in a cabin between Peskawa and Beaverskin lakes, c.1915, just off the doctors' route.

Lunch at Beaverskin Lake camp, c.1915.

Camps came in all sizes, shapes and comfort levels, as attested to by these two images of c.1898 spartan digs. The top photo was taken at Flanders Meadow while the bottom image shows the interior of Henshaw camp, both in Annapolis County.

A gathering of Milford House guides. Front row, left to right: John Lohnes, Horace Munro, Charlie Charleton, Lawrence Munro. The identities of the men standing are unknown.

Horace [Munro, second from left, front row, above], who ministered to our gastronomic needs with such unvarying success, was very clean about his work and at once on making camp, while Charles was getting the fire started, he would get soap and a towel out of his kit and thoroughly wash hands and arms. Then with great energy, but with the precision born of long practice, he would start his campaign with the frying-pans and kettles. Our stock of provisions, while clearly within the limits of practicability, was sufficiently varied to permit a choice of what we should eat, and Horace never failed to consult our wishes on the subject, usually with some apt suggestion which generally met our unanimous approval.

As we carried plenty of eggs, they formed the staple for breakfast, generally fried with a bit of bacon or a slice of ham, but sometimes deliciously cooked in other ways. These with fried potatoes, farina, buckwheat cakes with maple syrup and tea, coffee or cocoa, furnished an ample lining to start the day on. Our luncheons were much more informal affairs, taken wherever we happened to be at noon time, and as a rule supplied from the gunnysack containing the canned stuff.

Corned beef (a.k.a. bully beef) was a canoe tripper's staple. As the photo on the right shows, "the guides never lost their appetites [nor sense of humor] for trout."

But the important meal was supper, coming as it did after the trials and joys of the day were over, when we were best prepared to appreciate the result of Horace's efforts. Trout we always had, fresh, well cooked after half a dozen different methods. Our enthusiasm for trout, as food only be it understood, waned, but this was not true of the guides. The bread, either in the form of cornmeal, Johnnie cake or white flour biscuits, was baked in the folding reflecting oven in front of a bed of coals. Potatoes and onions were in steady demand. The meats included pork, bacon, ham, dried beef, corned beef and tongue, and among the canned provisions were soups, baked beans, peas, corn and tomatoes. The dietary list was completed by dried prunes, apricots and apples, by rice, raisins and a few other trifles.

Chapter 3
A Stern Unfruitful Land
by M.B. Miller 1911

We crossed Peblelugutch Lake and camped at the water's edge on the hardwood ridge, with Pescawaw Lake of the Keejeemacoojee watershed 300 paces away across the rise. We had had two hard days, which had fallen chiefly on the guides who had worked like Trojans and without complaint. The canoes had not been benefitted by being dragged over the shallow bottoms or by occasional collisions with rocks in the deeper places, and required some white lead to heal sundry scrapes and scratches. It was agreed that we should tarry at this camp two nights to rest up and get into shape for the heavy pull of the next week, and partly because the morrow would be Sunday.

We lay abed the next morning, all save the early-rising George. As before, the entire absence of mosquitoes added greatly to our comfort. The wind was from the north, cool and brisk, and the sky remained overcast all day. About 10 o'clock we started on a round of exploration of Pescawaw.

We found it to be a lake about three miles long, its slopes thickly wooded with deciduous trees with an occasional clump of evergreens. We paddled up it in a rather stiff wind, fished around the outlet of Poplar Brook, then turning, came back along the further end and stopped for luncheon at a lovely little cove where a white sand beach made a striking contrast to the rock-girt borders of the lake elsewhere. Here we ate boiled eggs and buttered biscuit and drank of the cold water. After filling the canoes with fir boughs for our beds, we followed the eastern shore to the outlet stream, fished as far as we could persuade the canoes to float, then took the trail a few hundred yards to Pescawess. Both lakes are drained by the Pescawess Brook, which runs into the Keejeemacoojee at Pescawess Ledges. We caught twenty-three fine trout, then paddled back to camp, took a lesson in fir bough bed making from Lawrence, ate a good supper, and shot at a tin can with the revolver, all to miss it until George in disgust knocked it off its perch with a stone.

"The Indians from Bear River, [one is in this c.1900 picture taken by Bear River photographer Ralph Harris], following the ancient pathway of their forefathers, may perchance come through on their way to Keejeemacoojee or Rossignol."

We were much interested in a wildcat snare on the trail over the ridge to Pescawaw – a bent sapling, a piece of heavy wire, and a cleverly contrived trigger. Lawrence, as a practical trapper, was familiar with it and told us that snares were always set on trails or pathways, as wildcats are apt to follow such open ways in hunting. This particular device bore mute evidence round about that it had succeeded in its purpose, as shown by bits of fur and torn and scratched bushes. In another place we saw where a moose had recently broken down the small trees to browse upon the tops. Twice during the day there came to our ears the reverberating, drum-like challenge of the ruffed grouse, while toward evening the nighthawks circled and dipped close over our tents uttering their plaintive cries.

We were up at 4:30 a.m. Monday and we were off before 7 o'clock. There was always a pleasant rivalry between the guides to see that the other fellow was not too heavily loaded, and Lawrence especially was particular over the correct balance of the canoes, thereby indicating the pride he took in having everything just right. We went across Peblelugutch, out through its deadwater, and on to the Little Shelburne. Almost immediately we commenced to wind and turn, and as the day wore on, the indirectness of our route became more emphasized. Observations with the compass gave most inconclusive data, but by estimating averages we concluded that we were moving between west and northwest.

Something over a mile from Peblelugutch camp brought us to Granite Falls, which marks the boundary of the sportsmen save for those venturesome souls who are athirst for the untrodden wilds. It is true that a few trappers go beyond. A moose hunter now and then gets into this stern, unfruitful land, and the Indians from Bear River, following the ancient pathway of their forefathers, may perchance come through on their way to Keejeemacoojee or Rossignol. But we felt all things considered, that we would not be crowded.

"It is not woods etiquette for sportsmen to carry anything on the portages beyond their rods and lighter belongings, but George and Gurney were getting so tremendously strong that they ignored formalities and worked off some super-abundant energy by shouldering the packs on two trips."

At Granite Falls, a long stretch of rough water over which it is too steep and rocky to pole, there is a carry which we were informed was about a mile long. The mile was there unquestionably, but we could not agree on just how long the "about" was. The guides made three trips and were occupied by that carry for two full hours.

It is not woods etiquette for sportsmen to carry anything on the portages beyond their rods and lighter belongings, but George and Gurney were getting so tremendously strong that they ignored formalities and worked off some super-abundant energy by shouldering the packs on two trips. I being lazy, kept in good form and caught fourteen trout, one weighing a pound and a half. As the weather was cold, gray, with a sharp east wind, this put me far in the lead for the day's catch. Thus are the righteous rewarded.

Beyond Granite Falls we had fair going with long stillwaters for the paddles alternating with short falls for the setting poles. At many of the falls were the most attractive trout pools imaginable. Here we were with a vengeance in the country of Lawrence's big trout, but nary a big fellow and mighty few little ones could we get up. We tried all the classic formulas to bring about a change of luck. We tried nearly all the flies in the book, dry and wet, but all in vain. Wind and weather were against us. We were in the midst of the angler's doldrums, "the day on which they wouldn't rise."

An Eddie Breck photo of Mi'kmaq guides Sam Glode (left) and Louis Harlow making snowshoes. Sam Glode (1878-1957) lived at Milton near Liverpool, Queens County. He started guiding for Milford House c.1905 and was the best known of the Mi'kmaq guides from Milton, some others being John Francis, Andrew Francis, Peter Glode and Mike Glode.

About noon, having covered approximately three miles, we came to a carry of a quarter of a mile. As we ate luncheon the sun made its last feeble effort to break through the clouds, but it was short lived, and from then on the weather grew steadily worse to finally culminate in a drizzling rain. By this time we were leaving the wooded country, evergreens were getting scarce, and only occasional clumps of stunted birches and maples were to be seen. We were entering the barren lands, close to the high open country, where formerly herds of caribou made their home, the so-called Caribou Plains of Nova Scotia. Apropos of caribou, Lawrence told us that in the fall of 1909 he and Sam Glode, an Indian, had guided Dr. Fales [facing page] who was interested as a naturalist in determining whether there was any of them left in this section, for fifty-five days off to the westward of our path in a search for them without seeing any or finding any signs. It is probable that they are extinct hereabout and the immunity granted them under the game laws has come too late to save these noble animals.

For a man of his stature, it is surprising this grainy newspaper photograph is the only image that could be found of Dr. Alonzo Cartland Fales (1869-1953).

Alonzo Fales was born in Nova Scotia at Victoriavale, Annapolis County, the second youngest of nine children. He studied medicine at Halifax Medical College before transferring to Harvard Medical School, where he graduated in 1894. Dr. Fales returned to Nova Scotia, living in Bridgewater, then Liverpool, after which he moved to Malden, Massachusetts, in 1897 where he became a renowned eye, ear and throat specialist with one of the largest medical practices in New England. Fales remained in Malden until 1913 when due to declining health he relocated to Middleton, Nova Scotia, residing there for 18 years until retiring to nearby Wolfville in 1931.

Throughout his career Fales escaped the stress of his profession by taking an annual leave of absence in July for 10 or 12 weeks to pursue his passion for big game hunting while his wife Mary Alice (nee Curry) visited relatives in Nova Scotia. From the late 1890s to the early 1900s he hunted in Nova Scotia, Newfoundland, Montana, Maine, Northern Ontario, Quebec, British Columbia, and Alaska. He once walked 114 miles through Alaska to Nahlin Mountain in B.C., his group reportedly being the first white men to hunt that area.

In 1908, he undertook a hunting trip into southwestern Nova Scotia with Lawrence Munro and Sam Glode during which the two guides called up 28 moose. A year later Sam Glode guided Dr. Fales to the McMillan River in the Yukon, a tributary of the Pelly River, giving credence to Campbell Hardy's assertion, "It does not signify whether he [the Mi'kmaq guide] has travelled through the same country before or not; he knows the direction and that is sufficient."

Alonzo Fales was also an ardent conservationist who was instrumental in establishing Nova Scotia's first game sanctuary. In 1925 he travelled the backcountry of Digby, Yarmouth, Shelburne and Queens counties, gathering "valuable and definite information on the Boundary Rock district, [the favoured of four areas proposed for a sanctuary] and pointed out errors in the maps which were available." On October 29, 1927, Boundary Rock Game Sanctuary, its original name in the planning stage, officially became the Tobeatic Game Sanctuary. In the early 1930s, Dr. Fales also lobbied for the protection of fish habitat and the restocking of lakes and streams to enhance the provincial tourism industry.

Boundary Rock c.1899-1910, served as the boundary marker for Digby, Yarmouth, Shelburne and Queens counties. Left to right are Edgar A. Hurlburt (1874-1962), Forman H. Hurlburt (1882-1933), Gilbert (Bert) Walton (1888-1971) and James H. Sabean (1855-1937). The many inscriptions scratched into the lichen indicate the rock was a popular stopping point, possibly for moose calling.

Boundary Rock, as it looked April 2011, cloaked in new growth forest. Like Jim Charles' Rock, many had looked in vain for the elusive boundary marker. The initial euphoria of discovery for this search party turned to disappointment when strands of flagging tape marking the site indicated they had been scooped, possibly by surveyors or snowmobilers. Still, the story of the search made for great listening on CBC Radio. Left to right are Paul Maybee, Alain Belliveau, Barbara Shaw, Colin Gray, Philip Moscovitch; Brian Braganza is on top of the rock.

"In places ... the channel was so narrow that one could step ashore." Bear River guide Ingram Hatt, foreground, leads sports Frank Hayden (in the bow) and Guy Victor Turnbull through such an aperture connecting Eighth and Seventh Lakes, Digby County, 1930s.

All afternoon we paddled and poled up stream, finding no special difficulties, but being disappointed in the fishing. On the bank at one place we found a record on a tree where the Barrio Lake party, who had been there ten days ahead of us, had noted catching in the adjacent pool two trout weighing two and a quarter pounds. The big fish were there, but not for us.

Two or three miles brought us to Dunbar Lake, or Pine Lake. We used the strong east wind at our backs by turning the ponchos into square sails and making it carry us over the mile and a half of open water easily and quickly. Incidentally the sail up Dunbar Lake gradually developed into an exciting race which soon brought to the surface quantities of latent talent and skill in masterly sailing.

"Kahfan and the country around it ... was a perfect picture of desolation – water, granite boulders and a gray, fast-darkening sky."

From Dunbar to the next lake, Kahfan, was close to three miles, over short stillwaters and rapids in a very crooked course. For miles in every direction stretched the open country with low bushes, and now and then stunted trees filling the swamps and huge boulders scattered as with a mighty hand over the higher land. In places the stream was just deep enough to float the canoes; at others the channel was so narrow that one could step ashore. We saw plenty of beaver signs, once a dam and twice large beaver houses. Earlier in the day we had noted abundant moose sign, but in this section it was not so apparent. Overhead we had seen a hawk with a trout in its talons, and had swerved from his flight a great blue heron, but the most interesting find of the day came later when Gurney discovered on a little island in Kahfan a loon's nest with two large dark brown mottled eggs it contained.

We came into Kahfan on its east side, then turned north to find the further pathway. This was as far as Lawrence had ever been. Horace had never even seen this lake, and Charles was not able to take up the guiding until we had crossed the divide into the Sissyboo watershed. Kahfan and the country around it, as we saw it that night, was a perfect picture of desolation – water, granite boulders and a gray, fast-darkening sky. We were cold, wet, hungry, and the east wind was high and piercing. Save for a few short, ragged evergreens on the little rocky islets, the country was totally bare of trees. Horace and Gurney took a course along the east and north shores to find the trail which we had been told led to the carry to Moosehead Lake, while the rest of us searched the west shore.

This search revealed nothing which even remotely might be construed into a trail. Lawrence, Charles and I then went ashore at the north end of the lake and walked up a low hill, past a fox burrow, to get a wider outlook over the surrounding territory. Some distance away we saw a stillwater bending westward which Lawrence felt sure led to Buckshot, a little lake which he had been told lay somewhere above Kahfan. In any event its windings apparently pointed toward an isolated clump of evergreens, and that meant wood and shelter for the night. We found its outlet into Kahfan and paddled up it. Several hundred yards from the lake and at an angle in its course we found the trail; at least, we hoped it was the right trail, marked by a stake at the water's edge holding in its split end a rusty piece of tin. But we were too intent on making camp just then to let trails or anything else interfere, so we pushed on toward the evergreen where we found a campsite which offered shelter, warmth and food.

"We found a campsite which offered shelter, warmth and food."

"It was a wonderful place to fish. One could wade out and get long casts up and down, and the trout rose to almost any fly." – *The Tent Dwellers*, Albert Bigelow Paine

Fortune decreed that we should spend two nights on the Buckshot stream above Kahfan. When we awoke it was still gusty and raining hard. Lawrence and Charles were assigned the duty of a scout to determine just where that trail of the night before went, and if it led to Moosehead Lake, to proceed further until White Sand Lake was reached. The latter lake was the furthermost point on the Sissyboo waters which Charles had visited or could recognize with certainty. The purpose of this was to avoid getting the entire party lost or far astray. The two pioneers, therefore, went off in the rain, each in a canoe, the idea being to leave one canoe at the other end of the carry to Moosehead if the trail proved to be the correct one.

Nettled by another revolver competition with results not a whit better than the one at Peblelugutch, I vouchsafed the remark that I could catch trout even if I couldn't hit a tin can, and vaingloriously offered to wager a dollar that I could go over to the main stream, catch a fish and bring it back in twenty minutes. Gurney took the wager with a degree of celerity which immediately awakened me to the true proportions of my proposition. It was 300 yards to the nearest likely place, the intervening ground was thickly covered with deadfalls, thickets and living trees, and then the matter of trout rising was uncertain, especially in such weather.

"Above camp the stream was small but for a while it was possible to crawl along against the current." This picture shows guide Ellison Gray of East Kemptville, Yarmouth County, with bark canoe (and moose quarters) on Buckshot Lake Stream between Buckshot Lake and Stoney Ditch Lake in October 1914.

I was given the time, and off I started at a lope. By dint of hard scrambling, abundantly penalized by scratches, I managed to reach the stream in good time. Then came the test. The first few casts were ineffectual, and hopes sank low as the seconds flew. Suddenly, close by the rock, there was a swirl where the silver doctor had flicked the water, and the song of the reel sounded the note of a big trout – entirely too big a trout under the circumstances. Then followed a short, sharp battle, in which the scales of fate hung evenly – most evenly, since the landing net had been forgotten. But in a few strenuous minutes the sturdy rod had done its work and the trout was steered into a little shallow cove and gently lifted ashore. Without removing the fly, trout and rod were seized, and the rush back to camp commenced. Bumps and bruises and shin-barkings passed unnoticed as camp was reached in glory of success. Eleven minutes was the elapsed time, and the fish weighed a pound and an eighth!

The two guides got in about 3 o'clock very tired and very wet, and reported that the trail was the right one and we could go on. In the meantime the rain had ceased and the sun showed a tendency to smile upon us. Whereupon I started out with Horace in a canoe with the view of exploring Buckshot stream up to Buckshot Lake, and thereby achieving the furthermost source of the Shelburne. Above camp the stream was small but for a while it was possible to crawl along against the current; but presently this way became impassable without a carry. We left the canoe and followed a moose trail along the swampy borders of the stream, then walked a mile to a hill high enough to give a commanding outlook. From this point we could see still stretching off to the westward bits of stillwater for probably two miles, but no Buckshot in sight. It likely was hidden by some little ridge.

Cofan ranger cabin (shown here in 2012) for some unexplained reason is not situated on Cofan Lake but on the Shelburne River near Sand Beach Lake. Probably built in the late 1920s, it served as one of several ranger cabins strategically placed throughout the Tobeatic Game Sanctuary, each within a day's travel of the other by canoe and portage. So is it Kahfan, Cofan, Couffin, Koofang or Two Fan? According to historian and novelist Thomas Raddall, the original spelling was Couffin – French for a wooden splint basket. In the native Mi'kmaq tongue it came out Koofang, and more recently "because some English-speaking surveyor misunderstood the sound, it appears on modern maps as Two Fan Lake."

Some days later, when we were talking over our adventures with Heman Crowell, he told us that we could have gone from Kahfan to Oakland by this route. From Buckshot Lake there is a carry to Clearwater Lake, which drains by the Oak Knob branch of Tusket running into Oakland branch above Bartlett's, and from Clearwater Lake there is another carry over to Cranberry Lake, which flows by its own stream into the deadwater between Little Dish and Oakland. Buckshot, Clearwater and Cranberry lie almost in a line between Kahfan and Oakland. He could supply no information as to the length or character of the carries, or tell us much of the intervening streams. It is highly probable that had we known of this route we could have saved time and distance by going that way; but then we would have missed the very interesting, though roundabout trip we took.

The next day was one of carries – five in all. It opened clear and cool, with the wind in the west and not much of it. The carry from Buckshot stream (700 yards above Kahfan) runs straight north over the barren divide for two miles to Moosehead on the other watershed. The trail is good throughout and was formerly an Indian pathway leading up from the Bear River region. On reaching the summit of the long rise, we had magnificent views to the west, south and east. Pine Lake and Kahfan and the communicating stream lay before us like a wonderful map, and the bare, bleak surrounding country was seen for miles in its picturesque solitude. Close at hand, the dry, stony ground was sparsely covered by tough, short heather, and monumental boulders had clinging to their sides dry, somber-colored lichens.

We were all carrying or resting from 8 o'clock until nearly 12, but by that time we were on the shores of Moosehead, ready to eat luncheon before taking to the water route again. Moosehead Lake, so called because of its fancied resemblance in outline to a moose's head, is nearly three miles long. Like most of these inland lakes, a colony of sea gulls had their nests on the great granite rocks which rose from the surface of the water at several places on the lake. As a rule, one pair of gulls have a rock to themselves, and the nest is a primitive affair lodged in a crevice on top of it and of just enough material to keep the eggs and young off the rough surface.

Enjoying some R&R on the trail. In the photo on the left, East Kemptville guide Ezra Gray playfully pushes away a sport's offer to enjoy a wee drappie. A guide's life could be hazardous as seen in the photo at right, where a woodsman is leaning on his elbow with his head entirely wrapped in bandages. All we know is the picture was taken in the Kemptville area of Yarmouth County.

Guide John V. Hurlburt (left) and a sport camped in the Tobeatic, early 1900s. Men of Hurlburt's ilk from Kemptville, Yarmouth County, knew the woods and waters written about here like the back of their hand.

Our course took us into a deep rocky cove at the northwest corner, and from there through three-quarters of a mile of winding stillwater. Then came a quarter-mile carry – two trips for everybody – followed by nearly a mile of rather broad deadwater, which brought us in turn to carry No. 3, also a quarter of a mile. By this time our inexperience in carrying packs began to count, and when, at the end of the next short stillwater, we came to a half-mile carry over a rough, slippery trail, we decided that one trip would be quite enough for us. This threw three trips on the guides, and the same was true at the next and last carry of the day, a hard one of a mile.

They have a saying in Nova Scotia in speaking of distances that a certain place "is a mile and a piece away," but the piece may be longer than the mile. We were deeply impressed by the soundness of the maxim as applied to carries. Of course, any trail seems long after a certain time to an inexperienced man carrying a heavy pack, and there is no doubt that going back light for another load shortens the distance considerably, but when all is admitted, there still seems to be an innate conservatism – I was about to say parsimony – in liberating land miles, which made us wonder if the standard length of a mile in Nova Scotia and in the United States might not be different.

Jim Sabean's moose hunting camp on McCoy's Ridge in the Tobeatic. In the top photo, the only two positively identified are Ellison Gray, standing in the centre holding a moose call, and Jim Sabean, seated, foreground. The man with the frying pan may be the cook, Len Morton.

According to Ellison Gray's grandson, Colin Gray, "These guys travelled from Kempt, usually across the Grayhide Trail to the West Roseway Brook hunting up through Jack's Savannah and up into the barrens on McCoy's Ridge all with a team of oxen."

Loaded down for a portage. On the left is Milford guide Ritson Longmire. On the right is an unknown Yarmouth County guide.

The strength and endurance of the guides was an excellent example of what trained muscles could do. Of course, all of the heavy packs were provided with broad straps, which went across the shoulders and chest and enabled the man to carry the weight mostly on the lower back by bending forward; but when on top of this main pack was placed another substantial bundle and he carried an ax or something of the sort in either hand, the aggregate weight was anywhere between sixty and a hundred pounds. To carry such a load far over a rough trail, stepping from stone to stone, or sinking half-way to the knees in crossing bogs or balancing along slippery logs, was a feat in strength and co-ordination of no mean proportions. Particularly was the handling of the canoes admirable, as a canoe is an awkward thing on the shoulders, especially in high wind or in the forest, and the weight not inconsiderable, the ones we used weighing 80 pounds when new. The part which fell to us, if we wanted to work, was to carry the lighter packs, together with the odds and ends. As to the latter, I estimated before the trip was over that I personally had carried the butter firkin nine thousand miles. The figures still look moderate.

"A canoe is an awkward thing on the shoulders."

"We were all carrying or resting..." Many sports chose resting.

About 5:30 we came out on White Sand Lake, a perfect gem, approximately two miles long and beautifully symmetrical in shape. It was the first good-looking lake since Irwin. In the main the shore was abruptly rocky, but toward the eastern end there were wide beaches formed of white sand and granite pebbles. We camped on the south shore at the end of the carry, having come since morning ten or eleven miles. After the evening meal was over we jointed the rods. A trout and a rise or two served and we caught enough for breakfast, when a passing shower sent us scurrying to cover.

Our camp here was one of the most satisfactory of the pilgrimage. The tents faced the north and looked out across the lake toward a charming vista of water, rock and sandy shore, backed by low hills, thinly covered with evergreens and birches. Once again we were getting into wooded country, though on our shore it was still bare enough. The water was very clear and had only to a slight extent the brownish tinge which all the Nova Scotian waters get from the many muskegs. The night was chilly, the morning clear and refreshing, the wind blowing in light zephyrs from the west, and just enough cloud effect to add charm to the cerulean dome.

After breakfast the guides white-leaded once more the scratches inflicted on the canvas covers of the canoes by the rocky bottoms. Within a hundred yards of the tents were the fresh tracks of a cow moose and her calf, showing that they had passed us during the night, and on the sandy beach of the shore were the tracks of two wildcats.

The close intimacy of canoe and camp had by this time made us well acquainted with the qualities of our guides, and we were fully prepared to subscribe to the statement that no party of visiting sportsmen were ever better suited in this respect than we were. Straightforward, clean-minded and clean spoken, energetic and resourceful, always cheery, always helping us and each other, never a cross word in difficulties, never any shirking of an unpleasant duty, no profanity or dubious stories – in truth, they may be characterized as gentlemen, and gentlemen in the best sense of that much abused word.

Horace [Munro], the leader, was about thirty years old, slimly built and of medium stature. His quick, cat-like movements in everything he did spoke of trained muscles and perfect co-ordination. He was the merriest of companions, constantly whistling or bursting into a snatch of song, or lightly chaffering with Lawrence or with one of us. He had a good voice and a natural talent for music; he seemed to catch the refrain of a song with the greatest ease, and we never did get to the end of his repertoire of popular songs. He might not know the words exactly, but the tune was always right.

Game warden Frank Miller (right) patches a canoe while sport Frank Hayden looks on at Wild Gardens Sporting Cabins on Sixth Lake Stream, Digby County, c.1930.

Lawrence Munro eventually established his own fishing and hunting lodge on the family homestead at Lake Munro, Annapolis County, calling it Forest View House and Cottages.

Lawrence [Munro], the youngest of our corps, was a constant delight. He was only twenty-three and long of limb and face. In many respects he was a true boy with a boy's love of risk and adventure, but with this ever-present phase he had many of the characteristics of an older man – the thoughtful consideration of others, a capital knowledge of the creatures of the woods, an almost innate sense of location and direction, plenty of common sense, and a splendid canoeman, the best among our men. Like the others, he had served an apprenticeship in the lumber camp and on the trail, but his especial aptness in observing the birds and animals had its origin in a wide experience in hunting and trapping. Furthermore, he was the possessor of a perennial font of whimsical humor, which never failed to raise a laugh.

Charles [Sullivan], the eldest, was the sturdiest and strongest, having a short, stocky, well muscled frame, which bespoke the great strength and endurance which was his. He, like the others, was always polite and willing, but he was more quiet and not as communicative as either Horace or Lawrence. Nor was he as adroit in the canoe, and always preferred to make a carry rather than to take a chance through doubtful rapids. In camp he was a yeoman for work, and tackled the hardest part of it with rare cheerfulness. He and Lawrence had spent the previous winter in running lines of traps for otter, mink, fox and muskrat, and at the current market prices for fur, this had proved far more profitable for them than working in a lumber camp, the usual winter occupation of the Nova Scotia guides. We followed

Weymouth guides Ned Sullivan (left) and Charlie Sullivan.

the excellent plan of changing guides each day, thereby securing the well-knit comradeship which is so important for a successful camping trip.

We started on the two-mile paddle down White Sand Lake as late as 9:30, shaped our course west by northwest in the face of a light breeze, and ran out of the lake into a winding stillwater. Almost at once we roused a loon from her nest. She dove into the water with a resounding splash. The nest was a rough, haphazard collection of small twigs a couple of feet from the water's edge in the low bushes, and contained two large eggs. After following the narrow stillwater for some time, we came to the remains of a burnt dam, relict of long gone days of lumbering. Around the blackened, rotting timbers we had to make a carry of a few paces, and it was here we started to catch the usual day's quota of trout. Near an old campfire we saw a bunch of porcupine quills, and later kicked over a part of the dried thorax. At once Lawrence, a perfect Sherlock Holmes in the woods, said that some French-Canadians had camped there. It appears that the French are the only people who eat "porkies," though Dr. Breck had warmly recommended the liver, nicely broiled, as quite a delicacy. However, any yearnings we might have had for broiled porcupine liver were offset by Lawrence's emphatic utterances on the subject. One time when he was lost in the woods he was obliged to take to a diet of porcupine in default of anything else.

"... scattered about ... we saw the whitened bones of an unusually large moose." There'd be a few moose bones lying around after this early 1900s hunting trip in Yarmouth County. Ellison Gray stands at right holding a birchbark calling horn.

The only exciting adventure of the morning came when we were paddling along over a long deadwater, when suddenly a crackling of sticks was heard in a little thicket just ahead. While we were hurrying ashore Horace and Lawrence commenced to "call." We heard the answer and caught glimpses of a cow moose weaving back and forth through the bushes. She was a large cow, but her coat was rough and poor. We heard a calf bleat two or three times, but could not see it in the undergrowth.

There seemed to be plenty of trout, but we caught none weighing a pound. By night the total catch numbered forty-nine. We lunched on a pretty wooded knoll close to the commencement of the carry to Sixth Lake Stream. This carry is on the route to Bear River by way of Sixth, Seventh, Eighth and Ninth Lakes and Lake Jolly. Near it was an old camp, and scattered about it we saw the whitened bones of an unusually large moose. Further back in the woods were the log ruins of an extensive lumber camp.

All afternoon we wandered down the pretty Sissyboo, paddling mostly, and getting through the rougher faster places without mishap though there were many times when the forward crew had to disembark. The west wind had freshened and was a nuisance when the winding course made it a head wind, while, when fair, the poncho sails were brought into action. Two or three miles before we reached Fifth Lake we noted the confluence of Sixth Lake Stream with ours, and below this, the Sissyboo was quite a sizable little river. The banks were beautifully and closely verdured. Rocks ceased to be as prominent a feature of the landscape as they were further up.

Life jackets were non-existent and many guides couldn't swim. When one old-timer was asked what he would have done if his canoe flipped over, the grizzled woodsman calmly replied that he'd sink to the bottom, then walk ashore.

We reached Fifth Lake after 4 o'clock, having traveled north by northwest all day. We were to turn right-about-face and go in a general southerly direction to the salt water at Tusket. We entered the lake near its southeastern corner, and immediately ran into a sea which pitched and tossed the canoes around severely. Taking advantage of all possible windbreaks on the shore, and paddling steadily at bow and stern, we first struck directly north out on the lake to round two long points of land, then turning westward and hugging the south shore, we bent our shoulders for a hard two-mile pull in the face of the wind. We passed several coves on our way, and saw afar off across the troubled water the deep bay, where the outlet lay at the northwest corner. Fifth Lake, while not in its best mood the day we saw it, is unquestionably a superb body of water. It is three or four miles long, and in many places over a mile wide; the many indentations along its shore line and the close forest which surrounds it, create a charming *coup d'oeil*.

At the western end of the lake we crossed a small cove and ran out of the wind into Sporting Lake Stream. A placid stillwater, which wound and wound through reed-growing shallows – an ideal home for the many ducks which frequent it – was followed by a stretch of stream with higher wooded banks, and presently, presaged by the foam-flecked current, we reached a short, rocky falls, and the first carry on this stream. Here we camped on the top of a steep embankment.

It was getting close to the stage in the trip when we should know whether we were astray and obliged to ignominiously turn back to get out as best we might, or whether we would be able to find Oakland Lake and accomplish our full purpose. We knew there still was a day's journey ahead of us before the crucial test, but we could not help wondering what the fates had in store.

We were up at 5 o'clock, and two hours later started upstream again. Scarcely a quarter of a mile had been covered before a carry of two or three hundred yards became necessary, but after that the going was fairly good for a couple of miles through stillwaters and easy little rapids. The weather was as near perfection as Nova Scotian weather can be – somewhat overcast during the morning, but clearing later in the day, with a light, soft breeze from the southwest, and the temperature of the air pleasantly warm.

Incidentally it happened to be one of those rare days when the trout rise freely and strike with that vehement certainty which gladdens the heart of the angler. When we reached the head of a long, peaceful deadwater, we struck such fishing as is seldom seen. With plenty of room to cast, with more than ample space for the three canoes, and with no wind, conditions were ideal. As for the trout, they seemed to be everywhere. They did not waste time over rising to the floating insects; they wanted flies, and the gaudier the better. And they got exactly what they wanted. Within fifteen minutes we took twenty-four, the majority ranging from 10 to 12 inches. At one time two rods were busily engaged with doubles and the other had on a single.

After so many trout had been captured and released that Charlie said we were catching the same ones over and over again, we were ready to move on. Through the woods for a short distance the guides carried one load apiece, and returned to pole and pull the lightened canoes up the shallow, winding rapid, while we walked ahead and discussed delightedly the details of that fishing.

Just a little beyond and on the right bank of the stream was a curious embankment called the Turnpike, which ran back from the waterway for over a mile. [See photo on page 186.] We climbed to the top and strolled along it for more than half its length. Had it been made for a railroad track by trained engineers the curves could not have been more graceful and easy. In many places it was over one hundred feet high, and across its level top it averaged about thirty feet. Its slopes were steep as though artificial, and throughout all the portion we saw there was not a visible rock or boulder, whereas as far as the eye could see on either side the usual rocky boulder-studded scenery obtained. Its contour and symmetry and conformation strongly suggested some gigantic working of the mound builders.

Three sportsmen portage on top of a "turnpike" running along Sixth Lake Stream, Digby County, in the early 1900s. Turnpike, a colloquialism for esker, is a sand and gravel ridge deposited from glacial melt.

A couple of miles of paddling and pushing brought us to a meadow stillwater, which was the scene of the most remarkable fishing that any of us had ever seen. Horace's sharp eyes had noted a little brook coming in on one side and had suggested the deeper water below its mouth as a likely place for trout. Sure enough, and for half an hour we experienced a blissful realization of fishing dreams. Almost every cast, no matter how carelessly made, meant a strike. With a trout on and fighting gamely, others would rise again and again to strike at the free fly until almost within paddle reach. This, of course, meant double after double. They averaged about eleven inches long, say three-quarters of a pound. Montreal and brown hackle seemed the best flies, but doubtless they would have taken any feathered fraud that day.

If any reader questions the splendid gameness of the broad-backed, hard-muscled Nova Scotia trout he had better hunt up that place and dissolve all doubts in a battle royal. Gurney buckled his rod completely at the middle joint, while my sterling rod commenced to show a suspicious kink near the tip. They were coming so strong that it was a temptation to push the fight a bit too hard and land the fish in order to get the flies back on the water. It was magnificent sport and the second experience exceeded the earlier one in size and numbers of trout, but could not approach it in idyllic surroundings. Somehow that day the ordinary fishing elsewhere palled, so that the day's record of 110 practically represented the results from these two places. Of these we only kept eight.

Trail cooking with a forked stick. Looks like the food may be precariously close to falling in the fire – a not unheard of fatality. Tappan Adney wrote c.1888, "It takes work and air to make a man hungry. We don't eat at all in the city. We mince and fuss and coax our jaded appetites, and in the end die of indigestion."

Shortly afterward the kettle was boiled over a fire of tiny sticks. After a hot contest, Horace finally succeeded in filling us up with buckwheat cakes. Then followed a brief snooze on the springy heather under the gratefully warm sun. Much of the going during the afternoon was difficult. Above the Pine Lake branch the stream was small, shallow, tortuous, in places overgrown with trees and bushes and bore on its face clear evidence of not having been traveled. At times we were all out of the canoes lifting, or cutting away some dead tree which obstructed the passage. In one place it was impassable and we made a quarter-mile carry through the tangled underbrush.

About four o'clock we came out on a small shallow lake filled from shore to shore with reeds and other water plants. It was called Russia Lake – probably a corruption of Rush or Rushy – and it was a great place for ducks. We saw several old ladies with young, and Lawrence and I tried to capture one of the pretty downy ducklings, but gave it up when tired and blown. On a large boulder was a gull's nest with the customary two eggs in it. Pushing the canoes through the reeds, we entered a sandy, shallow stream. A quarter of a mile of this brought us to the trail to Sporting Lake. The three-quarter-mile portage took an hour and a half and we were on the shores of a large lake, the most beautiful of all the smaller lakes we

Eddie Breck photos of an elaborate trail camp somewhere in the land of The Tent Dwellers.

had seen. Near the end of the carry was a trail at right angles to ours running off to the east, but where it went no one knew.

We should have paddled three miles southwest to the deepest cove on the south shore, but Charles, who was a trifle hazy on Sporting Lake, steered us too far to the west and we landed on the carry to Pine Lake. A search along the south shore was then instituted. Mr. Thomas had written down the directions for our trip at the dictation of Louis [Harlow], the Indian, but these were none too accurate at many places, and here, where we needed precise information most, they were articularly vague. However, by dividing the south side of the lake into sections, we covered the shore line methodically, with Charles showing by his activity that he felt the responsibility which rested on him. While on this search Gurney discovered another gull's nest, of which there were apparently many on the lake, and while the old birds circled high over head, uttering their raucous cries, he and I climbed a huge granite block rising from the water and found two baby gulls. With their down-covered bodies, grayish in color with dark spots, and their bright black eyes, they made a pretty picture of bird life as they shifted along a crevice in the gray rock which they so nearly resembled in color.

After considerable delay, Charles found the trail of another carry going south at the end of a deep cove, but it was getting late, so we pulled ashore, unloaded the canoes and started supper, while Charlie and Lawrence proceeded up the trail to see where it went. After we had done our part in getting the camp routine going, we adjourned to the water's edge, each man with grim determination written on his face. We were going to have a bath. We knew the water was cold, but such petty objection was lost in our greater need. It was not a pleasant episode, but we succeeded after a fashion. In the meantime the guides had returned with the news that at the end of the trail a mile away was Oakland Lake.

June 4 was an eventful day. For a week we had been traveling through a wilderness which was extremely deficient in sign posts or friendly policemen to direct us on our way. Once past Kahfan, the Milford men had only their well developed sense of direction and location to rely on; Charlie had done his part admirably, but he frankly confided to us that Sporting Lake marked the limits of his ability to guide, and even here he had been at fault in finding the right carry; while I could not aid until we had passed Oakland Lake. In a word, we all thought we were on the right track, but nobody was certain. The test was to come. We were about to plunge into the unknown.

The situation had one serious aspect and upon that phase George insistently dwelt with a pathos which was heartrending. We were nearly out of provisions, and if we did not reach Camp Marlett, or somewhere, pretty soon, it meant short rations, and short rations, to say nothing of starvation, would be a dire calamity to six healthy appetites like ours. An inventory of the larder showed that the coffee, cocoa, sugar, potatoes, pork and flour were all gone, and that nearly all the bacon and ham had disappeared; there were only six eggs left of all those dozens, a pound of tea, a handful of buckwheat, plenty of cornmeal, some rice, and enough butter, but alas it needed burial; while the canned stuff had purposely been used up long before in order to lighten weight on the carries.

As usual the camp was stirring shortly after dawn. The wind blew cold from the northwest, and there were a few dashes of rain, but the day turned out clear, cool and stimulating. We were getting expert on carries, and with all hands helping to relay the equipment and canoes, we were able to negotiate the Nova Scotian mile between the two lakes by nine o'clock. On this trail George saw a fine red fox close at hand.

We were then on the north shore of a small lake which bore not the slightest resemblance to my recollections of Oakland Lake, but Charlie was sure it must be Oakland, and it lay in the right direction. We paddled down this lake – which we afterward learned was accounted a part of Oakland and called by the Indians the Little Dish – in a west southwest course three-quarters of a mile to its lower end, then through a half mile of winding stillwater, and came out on a fine large lake, a mile wide and three miles long, lying northeast and southwest.

In a few minutes the mental images received five years before, when I had tramped up to the lower end of this lake and looked far off across it, revived and I recognized Oakland Lake. We knew where we were at last, and in high spirits we ran down it at a famous clip with the stiff wind behind us and the waves chasing hard astern. We were obliged to search for the small, inconspicuous outlet but found it a third of a mile from the lower end and on the western side.

Here came trouble. I recalled that I had walked up to see Oakland from the deadwater some distance below, but had not explored the stream between the two. Hence it happened that the rather easy going at the start of the waterway deceived us and we got degree by degree into difficulties. Some time later, after we had surmounted most of our troubles, we discovered a fine easy trail off to the left – the carry from Oakland Lake to Oakland Deadwater. The guides spent a couple of strenuous hours, dragging and pushing and lifting the canoes, before they were forced to give up and make a carry the remaining distance to the open water below. We did some fishing but the results were nothing wonderful.

After lunch the canoes were again loaded and we paddled from the upper to the lower end of Oakland Deadwater, probably two miles, over shallow sandy bottoms, and through a snarl of water lilies and other aquatic plants. All about us was a fairly open, gently rolling country, with short, tough bushes near the water, while further back scattered bunches of little trees of lighter green and finer texture, covered the rocky slopes. Now and then huge boulders rose like monuments from out of the water, or more frequently broke the monotonous outline of the hillsides. But in the main the country did not differ from that of other places where we had been.

Photo Album II
Gateway to the Interior

Fourteen-year-old Archer Turnbull (left) and guide Dube Rice paddle Sixth Lake Stream, c.1930.

Mi'kmaq guide Henry "Hank" Peters, originally from Bear River, Nova Scotia, passed away at the age of 96 in 2012. His detailed oral history account appears in *Guides of the North Woods*.

"Bear River was always a hot point years ago for guiding," said Henry Peters when interviewed in 1986 for *Guides of the North Woods*. "I remember years ago there were thirty-four guides in Bear River actually making a living guiding. Bear River is the gateway to the interior of western Nova Scotia. When you go nine miles back to Lake Jolly from Bear River, you could go through a chain of lakes – Ninth, Eighth, Seventh, Sixth – and when you got below Sixth Lake Stream, you could branch off and go to White Sand Stream, or you could go on down to Fifth Lake and go up Sporting Lake Stream.

"If you went up White Sand Stream, you could go on to White Sand Lake and then on to Moosehead Lake. Well, from Moosehead Lake you could portage over the heights of land and you would be in the Shelburne waters then, which are the headwaters of the Mersey River. From there you could go down the Shelburne River to a turn-off to Peskawa, Peskowesk Lakes and come out into Kedgemakooge or you could keep going down and come out at Liverpool.

"From Irvine Lake you could turn and portage over and follow another chain of lakes, and come out in the Roseway waters. From the Roseway waters you could portage over and come out on the Clyde River or the Shelburne River. My dad [Louis Peters] and I have taken all those trips and been through all that part of the country. I guided with him through there for twenty years."

HEADQUARTERS
FOR
Sportmen's Supplies

BEAR RIVER and its tributaries afford the finest Trout Fishing in Nova Scotia. It is also a Hunter's Paradise.

Fishing and Hunting parties supplied with **Guides** and **Outfitted** at Short Notice.

Birch Bark and Canvas Canoes always on hand for sale.

Correspondence solicited.

Yours very truly,

Clarke Bros.

Bear River, Nova Scotia.

This picture of Bear River's main street was taken in May 1899 by an anonymous American sport, who, with one or two adventurous friends, hired Mi'kmaq guides from the Bear River First Nation to lead them on a one-week canoeing and fishing trip into the Tobeatic around Boundary Rock. No doubt they outfitted at Clarke Brothers store (shown at left with staging in front).

A Real Trophy from the heart of the Big Game and Fishing Grounds of Nova Scotia

51 inch spread, 33 points of exceptional beauty in symmetry and colour.

That Picturesque Bear River is easily the best point from which to start on a Moose Hunt is evidenced by the fact that this splendid specimen was procured by our Bank Manager after only a few hours sport, within eight miles of the town, and in no way interfering with business.

One of the twenty-six brought out.

The secretary of the Board of Trade will be pleased to answer all and any enquiries. "Keep him busy."

Advertisement from c.1905 tourism brochure.

The next four pages contain photographs from a collection held in the Nova Scotia Archives depicting a May 1899 canoe trip. Close to train and ferry services and with a wealth of Mi'kmaq guides living on its First Nations Reserve, (shown here in 1899), Bear River was well situated to attract American sportsmen. Below are guides and their American sports at Lake Jolly, either prior to the start or at the conclusion of the trip.

Two canoes with Mi'kmaq guides and local sports from Digby – Major and Mrs. John Daley and Mr. and Mrs. Dakin (above) had a chance encounter with the American party and their Bear River guides near Sixth Lake, Digby County, which resulted in this group shot (below) at Frost Camp, a popular stopping point on Sixth Lake in the 1800s. Louis Peters, Hank Peters' father, is sitting on the wall of the log shanty. A young boy at the time, Louis would have been a camp helper and lugger on this trip.

Johnnie McEwan, centre holding a rifle, was described as the "dean" of the Bear River Mi'kmaq guides. McEwan advertised his services in a c.1930 tourism booklet. "When the rod and rifle are not in use there are other pastimes for the sportsman to do, such as taking pictures of wild game. Running rapids with canoes, bathing, and if you have an Indian guide with you he will learn you to be an expert shot with bow and arrow. Hair-raising bear and moose stories by the camp fires. I was very successful last season in hunting and fishing ..." Johnnie is in the photo below, on the right.

These images are historically significant in that other than being extremely rare they show woods travel little changed, if any, from the days of Campbell Hardy and the British officers 40 years earlier.

If Johnnie McEwan was the dean of Bear River Mi'kmaq guides then Malti Pictou, shown here during the 1899 canoe trip, was the patriarch, living to be 103 years old (1837-1940).

It was common for affluent citizens from the Bear River, Digby, and Annapolis Royal area to hire Mi'kmaq guides to take them fishing and hunting. One of these was William Sawry Gilpin from Digby, whose father Dr. John Bernard Gilpin (1810-1892) practised medicine for 40 years in Halifax and played such a prominent role during the Military Sport Tourist era that he was mentioned in Campbell Hardy's eulogy (see Introduction). William (1850-1885) was also a well-known sportsman, having a lengthy article entitled "A November in Camp" published in the November 8, 1883, issue of *Forest & Stream*. In diary format, he chronicled a challenging canoe trip of nearly a month taken under the guidance of Malti Pictou to the headwaters of the Tusket River, during which they endured snowstorms and temperatures of -5 F. Perhaps a similar trip is what killed him two years later, although no cause of death was given in the accompanying obituaries.

William Sawry Gilpin's grave marker at Marshalltown cemetery, Digby, Nova Scotia, 2011. No photos of him could be found. Rumour had it Gilpin died as the result of a moose hunting accident.

"The lately deceased William Gilpin, of Digby, was the son of Doctor Bernard Gilpin, of Halifax, an eminent naturalist. ... [William] aspired to none of that prominence in public or social life to which his large income gave him so open a passport; but was ardently devoted to the woods and streams wherever a salmon was to be killed, or a bear or a moose ... could be shot. ... His intense fondness and habit of every variety of sport cultivated till it became a 'second nature,' brought him into continual contact with the Indians, whose friend and patron he was to a peculiar and extreme degree. He would sumptuously entertain a dozen or a score of them at a time in his house; and not the least affecting sight at the sad obsequies was the crowd of dusky mourners, many of whom shed unwonted tears as they gathered around to gaze for the last time on the face of him whose like they would never see again. Living, he could paddle a canoe with the best of them. ..." (*Saint John Globe*, October 13, 1885)

"The unexpected demise of Mr. W.S. Gilpin, on Monday last, has cast a gloom over the community from which it has not yet recovered. In the prime of life, with an amiable and affectionate family, possessed of many friends, and with ample means at his command, of which he made generous use, he has been called suddenly away. The remains were conveyed to the cemetery at Marshalltown for interment, and were accompanied by a very large number of friends of the deceased. Some thirty or forty Indians, to whom he had so often proved a benefactor, were among the followers. A very touching evidence of the esteem in which he had been held by them was shown by their singing a dirge immediately after the body was committed to the earth." (*Digby Weekly Courier*, October 9, 1885)

A number of non-Native Bear River woodsmen guided during the Elite Sport Tourist Era. Two of the earliest were the Hatt brothers, Arthur (left) and Ingram (right), who operated camps (below) on Sixth Lake Stream, Digby County. In *Hunting and Fishing in Nova Scotia*, a 1930 tourism booklet published by the Dominion Atlantic Railway, it was noted that "G.A. Hatt, white guide, Bear River, has two log cabins for use of his parties in centre of fishing district. The charge for his services, including canoe and cabin hire, is $5 per day."

Guide Ingram Hatt (left) and sport Willard Read relax at their tent camp on Russia Lake, 1927.

Left to right are Dr. Guy Victor Turnbull, Ingram Hatt (standing) and Frank Hayden at Sporting Lake dam, 1927.

From left to right are sport Guy Victor Turnbull, Les Rice (1899-1967) of Bear River, and Les's father Dube Rice (1867-1945) in 1936. Note the gramophone horn Les used to call moose. Like many guides, Les was not big of stature but stood tall when it came to prowess and woods lore. At some point during the 1930s, Les purchased the Hatt camps and renamed them Wild Gardens Sporting Cabins, shown below c.1936. As business increased, Les carried out renovations and an expansion that ultimately resulted in four camps on the site – two for sportsmen, one for the guides and a cookhouse. Wild Gardens was lost to flooding in the early 1960s when portions of the Sissiboo River were dammed for hydroelectricity.

WILD GARDENS SPORTING CABINS

In the center of the Best Trouting and Big Game Country. Splendid opportunities for moving pictures of Wild Life. Guaranteed: Good Sport, Capable Guides and Comfortable Cabins. All for $7.00 per day

A REAL VACATION

Extra good fishing in May and June; plenty for eating in July, August and September. Bring your family and enjoy our famous Trout Chowder.

Further information may be had by writing

Telephone 38-14   **LESLIE E. RICE**

BEAR RIVER,   NOVA SCOTIA

Les Rice's business card, no date. During peak times he hired several Bear River guides, including the author's father Mal Parker, who travelled the woods with Les for many years guiding, hunting, fishing and trapping.

Two sports and their wives pose at an unknown camp with guides Mal Parker (second from left), Les Rice (by ladder), and Frank Parker (Mal's brother, far right). The man wearing suspenders and holding a can of Heinz spaghetti is Burton Frude, who cooked for Wild Gardens Sporting Cabins.

A very young Mal Parker (looking at camera, left) and two unidentified men clean up a moose.

Above left, Mal with an unknown sport after a successful hunting trip. At right, Mal stands centre, flanked by Dube Rice and Hardy Benson. Kneeling are, left to right, Earl Fancy, Ralph Purdy (Mal's father-in-law) and Frank Parker.

Building "Beaver Lodge" camp at John Paul's, 1936.

Rather than notching, logs were nailed into corner posts.

A temporary lean-to provided shelter.

Bear River teamster Murray Smith brought in supplies with his ox.

Frank Hayden, Les and Dube Rice – snow flies in November as the camp takes shape.

Les, Dube and gang lug in a camp stove on a sled.

Finished. Left to right: Dube, Guy Victor Turnbull (camp owner), son Archer, and Frank Parker.

Dube Rice, Francis Caswell and Les Rice pose to commemorate a successful moose hunting trip at Dish Lake, 1928. Dube had been a carpenter and ship's caulker until retiring in 1918.

Willard Read (left) and Frank Hayden at Dish Lake, 1927.

Bear hunting, 1939. Left to right are Dube Rice, Guy Victor Turnbull, Les Rice, Les's son Arnold (smoking a pipe), and an unidentified man.

Deer Hunting 1938. Standing left to right are Dube Rice, Frank Hayden, Les Rice, Frank Parker, and (seated) David Lindsey III.

A rustic Parker family portrait c.1936. Left to right are Frank, parents Alfred and LuLu Parker, Mal with his wife Geraldine (Purdy), and Francis. Many thanks to my mother Geraldine (1916-1975) who stressed the importance of schooling, especially the two R's – reading and (w)riting.

Fourth Lake Camp, Digby County, 1929. Les Rice often used other camps scattered about the backcountry for fishing and hunting trips. Nothing in the way of ownership is known about this cabin or the two on the facing page.

Preparing for the cocktail hour at Fifth Lake Camp, Digby County, May, 1929. Left to right: Les Rice, Mi'kmaq guide Joe Pictou offering a bottle to Dr. McGregor, Frank Hayden, and Earl Cossaboom.

Guy Victor Turnbull and May Turnbull relax at a cabin on Dish Lake, 1928.

Harbour View House at Smith's Cove near Bear River operated two camps at Sixth Lake in the early 1900s where summer guests were taken for fishing trips. A 1924 brochure advertised, "You may leave Boston after lunch and have your own trout for supper next evening at this camp [below]." Cost of a five-day fishing trip for two was $75.

In front of the "sports" cabin at Sixth Lake are, left to right, Dr. McGregor, Frank Hayden, Les Rice, Joe Pictou, and Earl Cossaboom, owner of Harbour View House, May 24, 1929.

Chapter 4
A Dash Of Peril Now And Then
by M.B. Miller 1911

At the terminus of Oakland deadwater, where it narrows and breaks as it runs into the woods, is Reeves' Camp. It is a simple, one-room shanty with a tiny porch, but that day it assumed high importance in our eyes as the first building of any sort which we had seen since leaving Maitland. We went ashore and satisfied our curiosity by prowling around it and peering into the windows. By this time it was after three o'clock and the matter of reaching Camp Bartlett and the supplies had to be considered.

From Reeves' Camp, indeed all the way from Oakland Lake, there is an ox-team trail which leads down the Tusket, sometimes near and sometimes far, to the first settlement near Hemen Crowell's home in East Kemptville. It passes close to Camp Bartlett. It may save frequent interruptions to explain that on former visits I had made it my practice to have hauled back to Bartlett's on the ox-team a flat-bottomed boat and camping material, and with my guide to walk the seven long hard miles. Except for the two miles near Crowell's the entire road was execrably bad, almost unbelievably so, and impassable for any beast of burden save oxen.

With the comfortable camp at Bartlett's for headquarters, I would make day's fishing trips up and down the main stream and along its tributaries; and when the allotted period was over the boat would be called into use for the return by the longer but far more beautiful and interesting waterway. In this manner I had acquired a moderately good idea of the Oakland branch of the Tusket. Twice I had gone on foot as far as Reeves' place and once to Oakland Lake; I had fished up the stream from Bartlett's for a mile or two and at isolated spots beyond, but never had attempted to follow the water route clear through. With this explanatory digression the chronicle of the day may proceed.

Two oxen haul four canoes over a rock-strewn trail somewhere in the backcountry of southwest Nova Scotia, c.1910.

It was decided that we should walk and leave the job of getting the canoes down for the next day. After turning the canoes over the greater portion of our equipment, we packed the food remains, the blankets and some necessities, and with each man carrying his load, we started down the ox road to Bartlett's. It was reputed to be four miles away, but I had been over it and mildly suggested that those miles were long ones. At first the road was not bad and we swung along it at a goodly gait, but soon it commenced to live up to its evil reputation. Over rocks and down gullies, across moose bogs, where we had to walk as though through heavy snow, on to bits of slippery corduroy, past watercourses, where a mis-

While the scene portrayed here is reminiscent of Camp Bartlett, this cabin, c.1936, was located at John Paul's, Digby County, and belonged to sportsman Guy Victor Turnbull (see page 205).

step meant a bruised shin or worse, through swamps and over high, hilly, gravelly land – in faith a choice variety.

Off to the east could be seen, now and then, patches of blue water of the Tusket, beyond it a hardwood ridge, while still further beyond were the Blue Mountains. Along this stretch of river pours in from the eastward the Oak Knob branch which has its source in Clearwater Lake somewhere near Buckshot, but we never caught a glimpse of it. Once we got off the beaten track in a vain endeavor to find a short cut which I knew existed somewhere. Finally after hours of trudging, with shoulders raw and feet sore, we forded the river, then Dog Brook, and presently Camp Bartlett stood before us. It had taken us three hours and it was unanimously voted that the four miles should be changed to six.

Never did that beloved old place look more beautiful. The broad stretch of water curving away toward the west, the brook on one side and the river with its tumbling falls on the other, the maples across on the point and further on the evergreens bordering the savannah as far as the eye could see, the fast setting sun lighting the sky into flame afar, and throwing near at hand lovely shadows. Commanding the scene on the knoll where we stood was the wooden camp with its primitive comforts. And best of all, Hemen had not failed us – our supplies were there, including fresh butter and eggs and several loaves of Mrs. Crowell's delicious bread. Horace immediately took advantage of the camp cook stove and the abundant new supplies to get us up just the kind of supper tired men need after such a day. How good it felt to crawl into those bunks on the soft meadow hay.

Our chief concern was to get the canoes and duffle to Bartlett's. As no one knew anything about the waterway from Reeve's down, and as I felt some responsibility by reason of having planned the trip, and, furthermore, as I had some curiosity about those portions of the stream which I had never seen, I decided to retrace those six miles and come down the river with the men. George and Gurney were muscle-sore and wanted to rest up, so they decided to keep camp and just potter around while we were gone.

The four of us were off by seven o'clock and two and a half hours later had reached the canoes. First we viewed the stream for a distance and found that a carry was necessary. Three hundred yards brought us out on a rock-studded deadwater down which we paddled. The easy going was short, and in a few minutes we were again in the midst of difficulties. There seemed to be enough water, but as soon as a rapid was reached the stream separated into three or four half-hidden channels, and, as Lawrence soundly observed, a greased snake couldn't float down such water. And with every rapid there came a thicket.

No one knew the country, and hence there had to be a reconnaissance with every stoppage to determine just where the next deadwater was and how best to get to it. To work like slaves to get through a rough place, then to load everything into the canoes again and start paddling to find that around the next bend the deadwater disappeared into another snarl, was the disheartening experience which was repeated again and again.

Once we went out to the ox-road three-fourths of a mile away, carried a mile and then got back again to the water; and once we cut a trail straight through the timber for a mile. To add to our misery the day was warm and the black flies scored unmercifully at every opportunity. By four o'clock we had made three and a half miles by water and were still up to our necks in trouble. We then took some of the dunnage in packs, turned the canoes over the remainder and walked nearly four miles back to camp.

Monday we awoke to a gray cold day which turned into a miserable southeaster during the afternoon. Charlie and Horace went out by the longer way to prospect the river to see if it would be possible to put the canoes in the water anywhere short of Bartlett's. Lawrence and the rest of us crossed the river near camp and took the shorter trail to the ox road.

On taking everything into consideration, particularly the report which Charlie and Horace made on the mile or so of river they had examined, we decided to make a straight carry to camp. Gurney carried the guides' blankets, one tent, the reflecting oven, and dragged in each hand a setting pole; George was loaded with his duffle bag, a tent and fly, and one setting pole; and my legs wabbled under my own heavy duffle bag, an ax, and the butter firkin. By going fifteen minutes or so and resting for five we managed to get into camp in about two hours, a very tired trio, and before another hour had elapsed the guides brought in the canoes.

We had mastered serious adverse conditions, we had met trying physical obstacles and had overcome them, we had shown ourselves to be men in the face of fatigue and discouragement. Nevertheless, we were not proud. We could not help thinking what double-dyed, green-headed idiots we had been not to have had Heman meet us on Oakland Lake with the ox team. But before this chapter of misadventure is closed, in simple justice a word of praise must be and hereby is bestowed upon willing, hard-working, courageous Horace, Lawrence and Charles. They were not responsible in the slightest for the situation which arose, but when we had gotten into trouble they had worked diligently and cheerfully until we were gotten out. To the next fellow who goes that way – don't forget Heman and his ox team!

"To work like slaves to get through a rough place, then to load everything into the canoes again and start paddling to find that around the next bend the deadwater disappeared into another snarl, was the disheartening experience which was repeated again and again."

Guide Ellison Gray and sport in front of Charles Reeves' camp, approximately two miles south of Oakland Lake on the Tusket River.

One of many unidentified camps that dotted the backwoods of Yarmouth County in the early 1900s.

After dinner the little cabin was brushed and cleaned to the degree of neatness we had found it in, Heman's birch canoe put back in its place, our own canoes loaded in water where they could float, and we were off. I, who knew something of the stretch of water between Bartlett's and Crowell's – a long fifteen miles – counseled that it would be wise to go part way and then camp, but the others were anxious to get the mail which was awaiting us at Heman's, and were inclined to push through. Little did they realize that fifteen such miles as we had before us could prove quite an undertaking for one afternoon's canoeing.

"[Lawrence] seemed to take a professional pride in running the rapids cleverly ..."

At the foot of Bartlett's long savannah we stepped out of the canoes, while the guides slid them gently through the headgates of the lumber dam, then came two or three rough places in swifter water, a longish smooth run, and we reached the place where, on the previous year, we had dragged the heavy flat-bottomed boat a considerable distance through the woods. This year, with the handier canoes and a more expert corps, we got through without much trouble by sliding the canoes over the smooth setting poles. Then came a mile and a half of easy paddling through Wallace Lake, another dam and open headgate, and on down the river to Pug Lake.

From here on we ran into a very winding portion of the river through many rapids, some of which were narrow and tumultuous, and all of which gave abundant opportunity for expert pole work. Lawrence enjoyed this work thoroughly and showed a dare-devil dis-

The Moose Calling Meadows perhaps?

position in taking precipitous falls which was exciting to watch but sometimes disconcerting to me. Several times when Horace would hold up to take a look at a particularly bad place, Lawrence would slide in and away he would go through the foam and turmoil. Once his pole stuck in a cranny in the rocks and for a moment he hung perilously near disaster, but he came through with only a little water in his canoe. He seemed to take a professional pride in running the rapids cleverly and sometimes when he had touched or scraped he would say, "I could go through that again and not hit anything."

All of this portion of the Tusket is very beautiful, but the weather was so bad with the rain and the cold wind that we did not enjoy it much. We traveled fast and well along in the afternoon we passed the Moose Calling Meadows, where on previous years I had been willing to call the halt to a day's journey to complete the remaining run to Big Meadow Brook next day. But we kept on.

Below this point the river was very circuitous, mostly in short twists and turns. Once in following a straight stretch of water, I ran into a channel which looked like the right course. There was some difference of opinion, but, deceived by the waves created by the wind, I felt sure it was the way until Lawrence and I had paddled up a long deadwater until we reached a falls tumbling toward us. It was hard on tired muscles, and harder still on *amour propre* to return to the other fellows who, in the meantime and by the exercise of a little common sense, had discovered we had gone astray by noting the direction of the waving eelgrass on the bottom. This mistake had put us on the Moose Lake stream, which heads up near Oakland, but at that time I had never even heard of it.

We found the continuance of our waterway far off to the left and thoroughly concealed until we were right upon it. Sometime later we came to a wooden bridge across the river. Here I rubbed my eyes and felt bound in truth to mention that I had never seen it. As a matter of fact we afterward learned that it was the bridge for the road to Rockingham, and it had been put there since I had been over this portion of the river. But that after-discovered knowledge did not help me. All confidence in my ability to guide sank to the vanishing point then and there. If it had been possible, I would have been handed my discharge forthwith.

The bridge and presently a meadow, where some one had cut hay, were evidences that we were getting near the settlement, but still no Big Meadow Brook. On we went with discouragement writ large on every face. Twice all of the others wanted to stop and make a camp in the rain and cold – and small blame to them – but I felt that the shelter of Heman's house would be worth every effort on such a night, and that we could reach it. Then came George's Lake and the wind almost finished us as we paddled straight into it.

Here one of our party, who was ahead, went ashore to indicate his feelings on the subject of camping, but I pleaded so hard for just a little more that I got it. Through a stillwater, down a rapid, and the familiar landmarks of Big Meadow Brook came in sight. We paddled up the brook a short distance, hauled the canoes out, turned them over the dunnage, and struck up the trail to the road. It was after eight o'clock. We were blue with cold, wet despite the oilskins, muscle-sore and almost starved, but the two miles to Heman's was quickly covered and six tired men were taken under that hospitable roof to be warmed, fed and made comfortable. Here we got our letters and the news of the big outside world.

Forest View House, Heman Crowell's guest house, 1910. The verandah is not yet completed on the new hotel, which replaced the original homestead that burned down the year before.

The main lodge at Birchdale Hunting and Fishing Camps measured 40 by 60 feet with a dining room and four bedrooms. Cabins were later added. Dr. Miller was a year too early to enjoy the impressive facility, which sat on 50 acres nine miles north of Kemptville at the end of Third Carrying Road Lake. Built in 1911 by Omar Roberts of Yarmouth, the property changed hands several times following his death in the 1920s, eventually serving as a monastery, Nova Nada, from 1972 to 1998. Privately owned today, Birchdale is now booked for retreats, workshops, reunions and weddings. Its story can be found in *Guides of the North Woods*.

A relaxing moment before the "great fireplace" in Birchdale's main lodge, c.1911.

It was with a supreme sense of satisfaction that we woke up under Heman's roof, warm and comfortable, with the good-hearted, story-telling Heman on hand to help while away a disagreeable, drizzling morning. It was agreed to go slowly until after dinner and we busied ourselves with letters telling of our safe arrival. Gurney in particular was anxious to get in touch with home over the wire, as his little boy, who had been out of sorts when we had left, had since developed typhoid fever, and while the accumulated letters of three weeks recorded nothing beyond the normal course of the disease – which by that time was nearly over – he naturally wanted to get the latest definite news before even thinking of going on to the sea. This could be done by sending a message four miles by team to Kemptville, where it could be telephoned to Brazil Lake on the Dominion Atlantic and thence go out by telegraph. George and I decided, in light of this unfortunate illness, to forego the rest of the trip unless the expected reply was reassuring, and to go home by rail without delay. As we could get the answer ourselves at Kemptville, we concluded to devote the afternoon to going down the river that far.

The important despatch, our letters, and two duffle bags were gotten off, and after a good dinner which included the great treat of one of Mrs. Crowell's incomparable rhubarb pies, all hands started up the road to the canoes on Big Meadow Brook. We had invited Heman to spend the afternoon on the river with us, and as the weather had partly cleared, he accepted. We had to slow the pace somewhat to accommodate ourselves to poor Heman's lameness, and it hurt me to see the crippling effects of rheumatism upon him. Our things were just as we had left them, but despite the shelter of the ponchos and the overturned canoes, some of our belongings had gotten wet in the driving rain. However, there was no chance then to dry them, so we loaded and got off.

Guide Curtis Atwood (right) from Barrington with a Mr. Ward and a good "mess" of speckled trout. The distinctively shaped canoe, owned by Tom Scott Sr. of Barrington, is noteworthy for its diminutive size, hardly in the 16-foot Fredericton category used by Dr. Miller's party. The unique native craft was built by noted Mi'kmaq canoe maker Joe Luxey, who lived during the early 1900s on the Great Lake Reserve in Shelburne County.

Alden Crowell (1857-1907), first cousin of Heman Crowell, was another East Kemptville woodsman and guide. He died of kidney problems, brought on some claim by years of wading in waist-deep frigid water during winter trapping season. Here he stays warm wrapped in a quilt while trying to call up a trophy moose in the early morning hours.

Heman Crowell (1856-1938) strikes a pose for the camera. Maybe he was hunting flying fish as there is a gun, creel and dip net but no rod. What a tale he could have spun about that.

"All afternoon we paddled or ran rapids."

The run down to Kemptville was pleasantly varied by the excitement of frequent rapids, a variation which never seemed to pall with constant repetition. There was fair fishing all along, but the trout were small compared to those we had caught in the waters less often fished. However, Gurney captured six, I got fifteen, and Heman himself, who was fishing with George's rod, took ten – all of which made a nice mess and were sent back to Mrs. Crowell with our compliments.

All afternoon we paddled or ran rapids; Heman palpably enjoying every minute, and we all delighted to see the good fellow's pleasure. At one place we had a trifling carry where the water sharply fell over the falls, twelve or fifteen feet high, but otherwise we stayed aboard throughout the run. We stirred up a number of mother ducks – blacks and sheldrakes – and watched them pretend to be desperately wounded while the young ones scooted for cover, there to disappear as by magic. One sheldrake had fifteen pretty red-headed ducklings in her train, an exceptionally large brood.

Speaking of ducks and ducklings, I am reminded of one of Heman's stories. It vividly describes a novel experience which happened to a widely known angler whom Heman was guiding over these waters. They were running a rapid and in coming through made a quick turn into the pool below. The speed of the boat as well as their sudden appearance served to carry them right among a brood of ducklings and the old duck. Immediately the fellows scurried for the banks and the old lady started the usual flapping, splashing exhibition. However, in her surprise and anxiety she failed to move away to a safe distance.

The fisherman, probably with no definite purpose in mind but merely because he had the rod in hand and most certainly without the slightest anticipation of the startling result, laid over that duck a clean, accurate cast which, on the instant recover, hooked a fly into one of those churning wings close up to the body. As Heman always says at this point – "My! Oh, my! Boys, then there was fun!" From the days of old Izaak [Walton, 1593-1683, author of *The Compleat Angler*] down it is likely that such a performance as followed was never before seen. Angling was carried into the third dimension, since the battle waged not only under the water but on it and over it. And oh, the sounds that went up from frightened duck and excited men! But tackle held and skill counted even under such astonishing stress and circumstance until finally – after hours had elapsed according to Heman – a bedraggled and dreadfully tired duck was released at the boat side.

It was interesting to note how the known distance by road was lengthened when the water route was followed. From Big Meadow Brook to Kemptville Corners was six miles, but the kinks and turns of the river doubled that distance. Part of the time we were near scattered houses and clearings, but mostly we were still in the unbroken wilderness as far as all appearances went.

Near East Kemptville, late 1800s. Left to right are guide Heman Crowell (seated on cartwheel), standing in front of Heman and leaning on the wheel are two unknown men (possibly sports), guides Dennis Crowell, brother Edward Bennison Crowell, Ezra Gray, and Alden Crowell (also seated on cartwheel).

Navigating some granite rocks in a birchbark canoe, 1899. Birchbark was a surprisingly resilient building material and could easily be patched on the trail using spruce pitch or tar.

    The granite rocks, which had been such constant features of the landscape since we had left Rossignol, had disappeared and were supplanted by a hard, grayish-green or grayish black shale. This occurred in ledges which, when tip-tilted across the river, formed rather precipitous falls, but the stream and the lakes had none of the great, imperishable gray boulders rising sheer from the water as did the granite section through which we had passed. From here on down to the sea this geological formation obtained and the effect on the scenery below was in striking contrast to the harsh, bare uplands, since with the passing of the harder granite came not only a softening of the outlines of stream and lake far and near but also a more abundant and luxuriant tree growth which still further heightened this effect.

    Just before reaching Kemptville we passed the junction of our little river with the Barrio branch, or the Long Tusket, as it is often called. It was quite as large, if not larger, than the Oakland stream. Under a threatening sky we landed at the Corners. Up the hill we trudged, with the guides carrying duffle bags, past the white church, past the store where they wouldn't sell tobacco because they were opposed to it, up to the modest but comfortable hostelry, where we proposed to stop for the night. Here the guides left us to return to the water's edge to make their own camp and we said good-by to Heman. The answering telegram entirely cleared Gurney's mind of worry and we all felt happier over it and over the thought that we could, after all, complete our trip as planned.

Not all the granite had disappeared as shown in this c.1900 shot of moose hunters picking their way through a rock garden near East Kemptville, Yarmouth County. Portage trails criss-crossed the Tobeatic of 1910 and were often used by guides driving ox teams, in lieu of paddling canoes, to replenish camp supplies and bring in sports.

Heman Crowell (kneeling at left) is the only one identified from this group competing in an unconventional tug-of-war called hog haul. Possibly originating from a traditional Native game, two-man teams locked hands on a stick and then tried to crawl toward a finish line while dragging the opposing team behind them.

The supper that night was made notable by the first fresh beef we had eaten for many days. Then came a sharp thunder storm with such a heavy downpour that we were concerned over the welfare of the guides and proposed to move them up with us, but the emissary we sent out reported that they were dry and needed nothing.

Somewhat later there came to our ears a curious chug-chugging noise which sounded familiar. In a moment there came in sight, *mirabile dictu*, an automobile of such an old design that it was difficult to approximate its epoch. Nor was that all, for we presently learned that its owner was a trapper who had on board a load of bear traps which he was taking as far up the road as the car would go, and from there go into the woods. Until bedtime we talked fish and fishing with mine host Walton and our only fellow guests, two visiting anglers from Connecticut.

In one of the lower rooms at the hotel there was a large map which we closely inspected to see if it gave any idea of the country through which we had been traveling. It was not satisfactory – none of the Nova Scotian maps are of the inland wilder portions of the province – but Mr. Walton, noticing our outspoken disappointment, got out an excellent outline map which was somewhat amateurish but still valuable to us since it was at once recognized as accurate. It showed clearly and correctly the lakes and streams of the Tusket watershed.

It is a current fact that while the sea coast and the land for a few miles inland are well known and the published maps portray it satisfactorily, yet there is a large part of the interior which is either not put down at all or so incorrectly drawn as to be worthless. We were much handicapped by this deficiency and repeatedly wished for something in Nova Scotia comparable to the excellent maps furnished by the United States Geological Survey.

Mr. [Del] Thomas had a large blue print of his own section but it was faulty with respect to the Shelburne River portions and showed nothing beyond Dunbar Lake. However, we had a copy of it, and with Mr. Walton's map of the Tusket, and with our own drawings of the country which intervened along the upper Shelburne and the Sissyboo, and still further supplemented by some of the printed maps, we were able to make a chart of our route from start to finish which fairly represented the waterways.

Whenever we met people on our way to the sea there was always considerable interest manifested in us and our little flotilla, and this was generally augmented when they were told of the extent of the pilgrimage. Here at Kemptville the camp of the guides, on the point at the foot of the village, was the center of an admiring group all evening despite the rain and hints to go home from the victims. While our friendly acquaintances from Connecticut felt it incumbent upon them to get up early to see our little craft and to witness the departure.

Horace restocked the larder at the store, and we paddled out on Pearl Lake, a large and very attractive body of water which had invisible portions beyond the further headlands. Our course took us southwest along the shore toward the outlet. Here Gurney unlimbered his salmon rod, the only one in the party, and started casting over the pool just above the outlet rapids. We were now on the part of the trip where we hoped to get salmon and could only by the merest chance pick up a trout or two. Nothing happened but it was a pretty sight to watch the fine clean action of the long, two-handed rod and the long accurate placing of the Jock Scott as every portion of the pool was carefully covered.

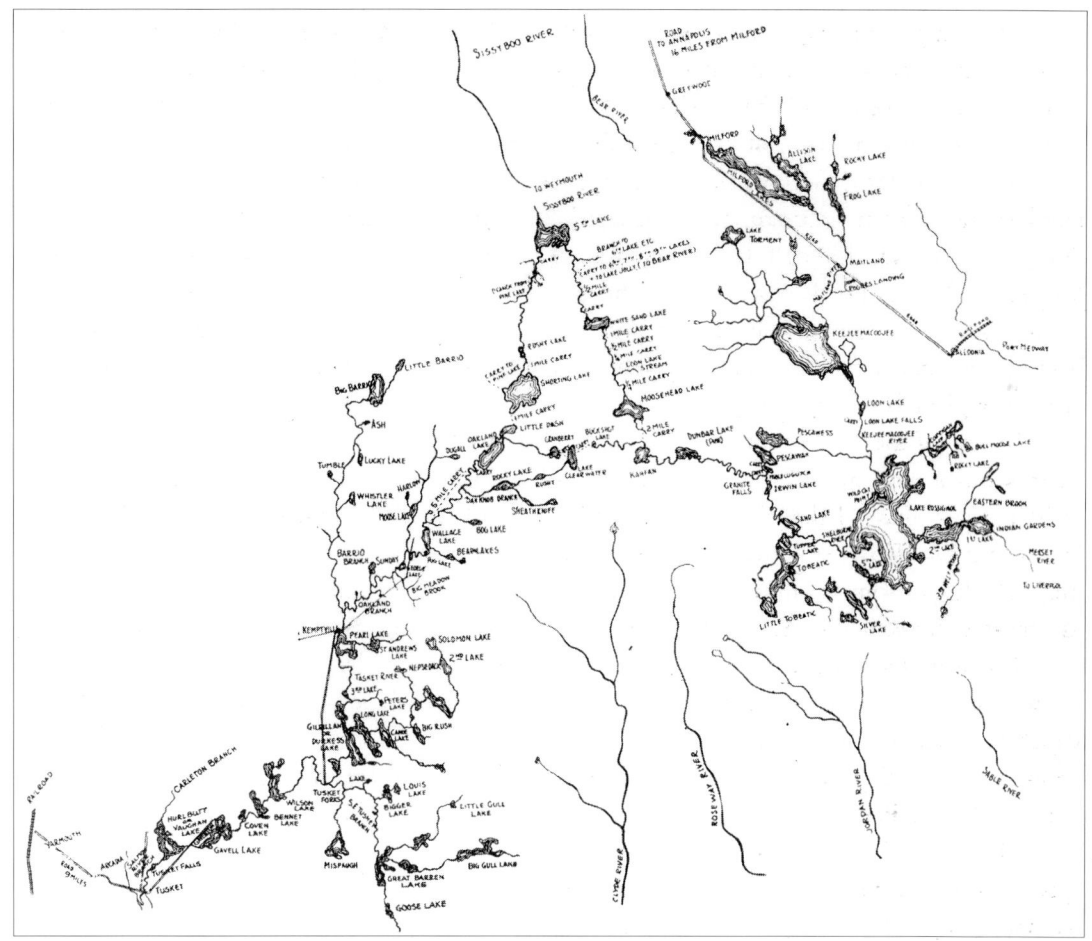

The original sketch from Dr. Miller's 1911 *Forest & Stream* article.

From Pearl Lake we continued down the main river, mostly south with plenty of water to run the rapids. Indeed, it was free running everywhere and the guides resorted to the skillful tactics we had observed on the Keejeemacoojee except they seldom used the pole, mainly relying on the paddle in the swift water. It was highly exhilarating to coast down the dark, curling, uneven hills of water, swept by a quick turn of the paddle from the hidden rocks, occasionally taking in a few drops over the bow at some unusually sharp declivity, but always getting through the rushing, roaring water unscathed.

Charlie had driven logs on the river and knew the bad places, but our Milford guides had never seen any part of it. However, there was little to choose between them when it came to quickness of eye in determining the nature of the falls and sureness of hand in avoiding dangers. Of course, running free through the white water solely with the paddle increased the chance of capsizing very considerably if anything went wrong or judgment was faulty, which was not the case with the slower method of dropping down bit by bit under the control of the setting pole, but with the good volume of water which we had the paddle was the only means thought of by our high-spirited, excitement-loving guides. And what cared we for a dash of peril now and then?

"Running free through the white water solely with the paddle increased the chance of capsizing very considerably if anything went wrong or judgment was faulty."

At one place called the Five Branches we three men were put ashore to soberly walk while the guides ran the lightened canoes down a long, steep chute made by the lumbermen for the logs. Each man came through at a terrific rate which was thrilling to watch; each man took in some water half way down where a heavy wave broke, but all came out triumphant. In going down stream in shallower, smaller waves, the bow paddle can often aid the progress of the canoe by occasionally lifting his end or by pushing the prow past the rocks and so keep it in the current, but in the powerful, heavy rapids of the larger rivers he had better – if he has a family – sit tight and leave the matter wholly in the hands of the Lord and the expert at the stern.

At Bad Falls, made by a long succession of jutting ledges, we made a carry and boiled the kettle. Even here the intrepid Lawrence showed some inclination to attempt the clearly dangerous feat of running through in the canoe, but he was effectually curbed when the rest of us threatened to tie him down hand and foot. As the day wore on the low gray clouds broke away and the evening came on cool. There was not quite as much pitch to the falls below the Bad Falls as there had been further up, but nevertheless there was enough to make us take notice.

Once in awhile we would idly cast a fly over some particularly attractive patch of water, but we caught practically nothing, save a few little salmon which showed in miniature the splendid characteristics of their larger relatives by repeatedly going out of the water in the most enlivening fashion.

The guides took every opportunity to demonstrate their skills running rapids.

In the middle of the afternoon we crossed a large pond which Charlie said was Third Lake and shortly beyond it we came out on Durkess Lake, also called Gilfillan Lake, a long, narrow, very beautiful lake with a single picturesque island near its lower end. On both of these lakes we saw a salmon net, which roused us to wrathful indignation. Wholly apart from any sportsmanlike feeling over such ignoble practices as applied to noble fish, we knew they were illegal as the law is clear upon the subject and specifically forbids the setting of salmon nets above the tide. We visited each in turn, pulled them up to see if any fish had been captured, disarrayed them thoroughly, but hardly dared to visit the proper penalty upon the miscreant owner by destroying them.

Approaching the lower end of Durkess Lake, where it debouches toward its outlet on the west, we saw a green canvas canoe drawn up on the rocks, and nearby a white tent gleaming amid the trees on a pretty grassy knoll just opposite the rapid commencement of the Indian Falls. We all went ashore and were cordially greeted by C.C. Richards, of Yarmouth, and his friend, Mr. Suttie. They were camped there for a turn at the June run of salmon. Our attention was immediately drawn to a little low gig nearby. It was fitted with a couple of light iron cradles lined with carpet and the purpose of this ingenious vehicle was to carry the green canoe.

Wellie Brown, shown here, guided at Milford House for 60 years. Some guides could count on 115 days of work a year during the busy decades of the teens, twenties and thirties. Brown would often be gone for three weeks at a time, then return to a rendezvous point, change parties and clothing, pick up supplies and go right back into the woods for another three weeks.

A much easier way of portaging a canoe. "He could bring his car within a mile or so of his camp and leave it in a barn. Could anything have been more ideal?"

Mr. Richards told us that he had purchased the pretty knoll and two or three acres of adjacent land from the Indian owner and thereby had secured the top salmon pool on the river. Whenever the spirit moved him – and I fancy from the gleam in his eyes that the movements came with sufficient frequency – he would get out his automobile, load on it his camping outfit and a similarly minded friend, and towing the gig with the canoe lashed fast, run the twenty-four miles up from Yarmouth. He could bring his car within a mile or so of his camp and leave it in a barn. Could anything have been more ideal?

Mr. Richards' tent was neatness itself and its perfect appointments were admirable. The light folding cots, the little table with a cribbage board upon it, the tiny camp stools, and particularly the collapsible sheet iron stove with its telescoping stove pipe extending through an asbestos-protected opening in the roof of the tent, all indicated a tent dwelling style quite superior to our own.

Mr. Richards gave us some useful hints as to where we might fish for salmon, indeed, wanted us to stay and try our luck on his pool – but the shadows were lengthening across the water, so we pushed on. We were in the current of Indian Falls as soon as we moved away from the shore, but we had no trouble and wasted no time in running through the half-mile of rough water. Then came a stretch of gentler current, another falls of short length but considerable momentum where a picturesque old man was dipping for gaspereau, still

A tent camp in the Tobeatic c.1910, with the river "sweeping in a generous curve in front."

another reach followed by some boisterous water, and we swung around a bend to haul ashore at Tusket Forks. Through the field we walked to the only store, interviewed the pretty dark-eyed girl in charge, whose tongue was just as nimble in French as in English, listened to the soft dialect of the local "habitants," telephoned to Yarmouth and arranged for teams to meet us two days later at Tusket, and then paddled across the river to the island opposite.

Here we pitched camp on the most delightful spot imaginable – a high slope, the blue river sweeping in a generous curve in front, the ground level and clothed with fine grass, and the whole sheltered by a magnificent grove of spruce and pine and fir. Under the trees stretched away long cathedral-like aisles carpeted with pine needles, while in the open spaces the newly spread fronds of ferns were gently waving in the soft breezes.

Across the swiftly flowing river was the scattered village of Quinan, or Tusket Forks, populated entirely by picturesque French Canadians, soft spoken descendents of the primitive Arcadians [Acadians]. Evidently the camp site was a favorite picnic ground, for there was all ready for us a substantial rough board table, carved with the initials and queer French names of rustic swains and maidens. But no bottles or empty cans marred the lovely prospect. A stone's throw away was a salmon pool and just before dusk a lone fisherman came out and cast leisurely over it for awhile.

"A tent dwelling style quite superior to our own." Note the small barrel tent stove.

After the dishes were washed and the tents arranged for the night, the guides got out from some mysterious place in their tiny kits, clean collars and neckties and paddled across to the village. We didn't ask them where they were going – maybe it wouldn't have done us any good if we had – possibly, after all, that pretty girl wasn't so communicative after business hours.

Another of a guide's myriad chores – washing up the dishes. Pictured are Art and Tom Canning, Irving Lake Dam, c.1915.

As the conclusion of the trip neared, the end of portages would have been a welcome respite.

Chapter 5
Yearning For Civilization
by M.B. Miller 1911

The morning dawned on one of those rare clear, crisp days which we had learned to highly value on a trip beset by so much rain. There was no great incentive to make an early start, since we had traveled eighteen miles the day before and that much more would easily take us into Tusket, but the usual program was followed and we were again moving by eight o'clock.

At Tusket Forks the Southeast branch pours into the main stream considerable water, so that our little river was materially increased in size and volume below this point. Presently we turned to the westward, then resumed the southerly trend of our journey.

The first lake of the day was Wilson's Lake, a long irregularly shaped body of water, the upper portions of which we could not see. We passed under a bridge just before we reached it, through a short rapid, and across the lake not far from the lower end. Then followed a series of rapids and Bennett's Lake. This we also crossed near its lower end.

A short run brought us to a long pitching falls where we came upon the rear drive of two and a half million feet of logs which were being worked down the river from the Barrio branch to the mill at Tusket. We had a fine opportunity to see a large drive in actual operation and to watch the clever, strenuous work of the lumberjacks. When we came up the men were pushing and pulling scattered logs into the boom which held the tail of the drive. As soon as they saw us, two men quickly made a way for us, and by stepping on one of the chained logs of the boom, sunk it enough for us to slip over. We then ran down the rapids a short distance to where the drive boss and several men were awaiting the starting of the logs from above.

The costumes were picturesque in the extreme – heavy low shoes with the soles thickly studded with long, sharp, spine-like hobnails, thick woolen stockings, knee breeches, flannel shirts, and big hats. The contrast in physiognomy between the drive boss, a tall sandy Scot, the swarthy French-Canadians, and the copper-hued Indians, was striking. Each man was armed with a strong steel-shod pole or heavy peavey. They were an alert and well set-up lot – forsooth a log drive is no place for dullards or weaklings. Their quiet manner, their genial greeting, their instant, cheerful aid in helping us through the logs, all rather gave the lie

Woods crew from Kemptville, Yarmouth County, c.1900. Back row, left to right: Ellison Gray, Loren Gray, Sam Morton, Jud Gray, Maurice Prosser, Amos Travis, Obid Hamilton. Front row, left to right: Felton Travis, Arthur Bower, Frank Prosser, John Bower, Len Morton, Charlie Prosser, ? Patterson.

to the generally accepted idea of the evil character of lumberjacks, at least as applied to this section.

We had hardly gotten off before the logs came tumbling down the rapids after us. Heavy logs in white water are not pleasant competitors in a canoe race, but we made it safely and slipped aside at the foot into a little cove just above where the collected logs were held by booms until a favorable wind permitted them to be warped across the lakes below. There were several acres of these logs ahead, completely filling the river and with no appreciable passageway in sight, while the moving logs were shooting in fast upon them.

A young fellow named Armstrong, one of two brothers who had the contract to deliver this drive at Tusket and whom we had seen part way up the rapid working with his men to prevent the moving logs from lodging, noticing our predicament, jumped on a passing log, and with nothing to balance him but his setting pole, rode down the rapids to our aid. That feat of standing erect on a tumbling, rolling stick of timber running through the falls was no mean one, but he followed it up by a splendid exhibition of agility and dexterity, as he made a channel for us to follow, which was a perfect revelation.

Running over the bobbing logs with sureness of step and remarkable quickness he would strike the right log with the pole and push it away, or walking a log with his rough shod shoes, he would move it and those adjacent far enough back to let us by. Back and forth at full speed, never missing foothold, never wasting an effort, he gradually worked a passageway, and finally when the confining boom was reached he stood upon one end of a

Two guides and their sports approach a log driving crew on the Tusket River in the early 1900s. Similar boats – flat-bottomed punts for navigating shallow water – were used for salmon fishing on several Nova Scotia rivers.

chained log until we had slipped over it, and then, wishing us a good day, turned back to his work. With his superbly developed figure, pink cheeks, blue eyes, and curly hair, he made a fine upstanding picture of a man. Even our guides, all of whom had worked upon the drives, admitted that he was "a mighty clever man" and went into a long discussion as to whether they had ever seen a better one.

Lunch disposed of, we wandered out upon Gavell Lake, a long, cloverleaf-shaped lake divided by capes of land on either side, one of which was occupied by the camp of the log drivers. At the foot of this lake we came to the little hamlet of Gavellton, where an iron bridge crosses the river. Here we went ashore, as it was a warm, lazy afternoon and we were in no hurry, and loafed a bit while Charles went off with his paddle under his arm – he never went ashore without carrying that precious paddle – to find out whether the log drive which we were approaching in the next lake was quiet or moving.

Presently we started again, passed under the bridge and into the stretch of rapid water which runs several hundred yards and finally dumps into a particularly swift, precipitous, and rather ugly fall. At the worse part of this fall the water curls and tumbles in heavy, roaring volume, and the proper, craftsman-like way to take it was to give the paddle a sudden and strong twist just as the crest was reached, thereby missing a treacherous rock which was covered by enough water not to show but which constituted a very real danger to canoes.

Charlie ran it beautifully, as did Lawrence, and neither canoe took in more than a cupful of water, but in some way Horace went too straight. In an instant the canoe was nearly half full, but the speed was so great that it staggered on through the swirls and foam and came out on Vaughan Lake without sinking.

Vaughan Lake is a fine large lake shaped somewhat like a Maltese cross. At its northwest corner comes in the Carleton branch of the Tusket. Across the lake near its outlet we found a quiescent drive of logs, held above and below by long booms; through this tangle of timber we were obliged to work our own channel unaided. Just below a pretty cabin was the small Tusket Lake, and across it we paddled to run ashore at the head of Tusket Falls.

Our attention was soon directed to the gaspereau fisherman, two of whom were close by, while others we could see further down the falls. We walked out a light trestle to visit the nearest stand and were welcomed by its occupant, Mr. Brayne, who let us sit and watch him, while he told the story of the gaspereau.

The method employed in this curious form of fishing is substantially the same all along the Tusket. During the low water of the late summer a short sluice is built of smooth logs along the edge of a rapid, and sometimes when well out in the current a little wing of logs and stones is added to direct the fish into the narrow channel. Through the sluice way the water rushes at a depth of three or four feet. During the spring and early summer countless numbers of the gaspereau, or kyack or alewives, as they are variously called – a member of the herring family – run up the Nova Scotian rivers to spawn.

The fisherman sits by the side of the sluice and using a large dip net with a six-foot handle sweeps down the current toward the on-coming fish. Apparently they make their rushes up stream in little schools, as the dipping net would go through many times without result, then up would come anywhere from three or four to a dozen wriggling, silvery fish. These are dumped into the flat-bottom end boat always within reach, and usually the next scoop, if quick enough, takes a few stragglers from that school. The dipping proceeds with monotonous regularity, a minute or two intervening, hour after hour.

Mr. Brayne, who not only dipped himself but also dealt in the catch of others, told us that, in the main, gaspereau are iced and sold to the deep-sea fishermen to be used for bait, especially for halibut, and that they brought about seventy-five cents a hundred. An average day's catch would run from one to three hundred fish, though sometimes as many as fifteen hundred were taken by one man.

At several places on the lake were anchored salmon nets and on the next morning's run below the falls we saw a good many more. Those above were there through a rather free interpretation of the law, since it is a very rare occurrence for the tide water to back far enough up the falls to flow into the lake. Day and night these deadly traps awaited the moving salmon, and from their number and distribution we marveled that enough fish got through to propagate their kind, to say nothing of enough to entertain sportsmen. It is true that about thirty-six hours each week the nets are supposed to be lifted, and it must be due to this salutory restriction on the market fishermen that any of these lordly fish are left at all.

The St. Mary's River, Guysborough County (shown here), is one of several Nova Scotia rivers with a long history of salmon fishing, others being the Margaree, Mersey, Medway, Barrington, Jordan, Clyde, Roseway, Salmon, and Annapolis.

The Margaree River on Cape Breton Island has been visited by salmon fishermen since the mid-1800s. Nova Scotia salmon rivers are relatively quiet today compared to the 1920s, when it was claimed the Mersey had 75 tents along its banks at any given time catering to American sports.

The whole matter of netting seemed to us extremely unfortunate and based on a penny-wise-pound-foolish policy. Every one of the little Nova Scotian rivers are natural salmon streams, and with the abolishment of netting, the insistence on fish ladders, and some wise supervision they could be made as interesting to fly-fishermen as the Newfoundland waters. Taking into consideration the easy access from the United States, the full development of the possibilities of these rivers could readily make every salmon a hundred times as valuable to the provincial people as it is now.

That night we had our last meal as an unbroken party. George and Gurney, who had been showing slight indications for a day or two that thoughts of the flesh pots of Egypt were coming to the fore, had arranged with Mr. Brayne to sleep and breakfast at his house, but I, who never yet have been surfeited by the joys of the woods, postponed the inevitable for another night at least.

The next morning I was awakened by unseemly chatter outside the tent. Turning out, I learned that a salmon had met his doom in the net which was stretched in the current out near the boom. Even as I stood at the tent flap and gazed across to the net another salmon struck it, and for a brief while the violent convulsive bobbing of the corks showed the tragedy which was being enacted underneath.

An unidentified riverside camp with two salmon beauties on display.

Presently from somewhere up the lake came the rhythmic sound of oarlocks and the owner of the net rowed down to secure his spoil, then coming our way and landing, he laid upon the grassy sward two fine fresh-run salmon, one of nearly fifteen pounds, and the other weighing about twelve. He didn't say anything. He didn't need to. The color and sheen and graceful shapeliness of those splendid fish were potent magic far beyond his powers. Unmindful of the distance and the trouble entailed, and perhaps of some other things, I determined to take one of those beautiful fish home with me, and for a paltry sum the larger fish became my property. The guides, with no greater resistance to temptation, took the smaller one at bargain rates, while later in the morning below the falls even Gurney, he of the salmon rod, fell from grace and bought a salmon.

Up the road through the drizzling rain – for it had commenced to rain about daybreak – I carried my prize to Mr. Brayne's house, there to find my companions clad in the garb of the city, though some concession to the weather might be noted in the superimposed oilskins. Truly the yearn for civilization was hard upon them! The matter of transporting the salmon was laid before Mr. Brayne, whereupon with hammer and saw he quickly made an admirable box neatly fitted with a handle, and then, sending his small lad off to the meadow for moss and to the ice-house for ice, the three of us securely and, as it afterward proved, successfully, packed the salmon for the long journey home.

This Milford guide would have earned his $2-a-day wage lugging all this gear – plus the canoe.

In the meantime the guides carried the heavy things to the foot of the falls and ran the canoes through while we stood on the porch and watched for the last time their clever tactics. We were now on tide water with the ocean only a few miles away. The river wound considerably, was not particularly interesting, and presented no difficulties, except we had some trifling trouble getting over another log boom. Presently there came in sight the iron bridge of the Halifax and Southwestern Railway, and here we stepped ashore for the last time from those sturdy little craft which had carried us so well from Roger's Landing through the wilderness to Tusket.

We had a long and dreary wait that rainy day before the teams for Yarmouth could be hurried over for us. The general store soon ceased to entertain us, the great saw-mill where rough logs were seized and turned into boards as in the twinkling of an eye only served to hold our interest for a little while. The only pleasant feature of that long wait was the good dinner we got at a charming old-fashioned house kept by the widow of a sea captain, where the atmosphere of gentle refinement and perfect courtesy made us feel like honored guests.

Finally two three-seated buckboards arrived, and while the six men of our party and the driver occupied one, our equipment was carried on the other. The arrangement for the canoes was ingenious and so satisfactory that no time was lost in transporting them. Two were placed on cross pieces of scantling resting on the seats. This brought them over the wheels, but well above them. The third was placed on top of the back seats and all three were securely lashed. This left plenty of room for all the other dunnage on the body of the wagon.

The drive of nine miles to Yarmouth over a good road was soon accomplished, and it was not long before we were settled at the hotel. I shall not dwell upon the joy – the perfect, blithering, blissful joy – which we took in the hot baths, the clean clothes, the comfortable

Loading up – end of the line. "One does not go through that final ritual without a little sentiment – a little tugging about the heart." – Albert Bigelow Paine, *The Tent Dwellers*

Eugene Freeman with a bevy of Rossignol beauties, c.1918 – "the wonderful, wild, abounding Nova Scotia trout." – Albert Bigelow Paine

Dr. Miller and his fishing buddies would have been envious of the mode of travel afforded the sportsmen featured in this c.1912 postcard from Yarmouth.

surroundings, the good beds, and last, but not least, the excellent meals at real tables with white napery and trim waiting maids.

The following day, June 10, three guides were seen off on the "Flying Bluenose," with their knuckles sore from hearty hand grips and their ears ringing with praise and appreciation, and along in the afternoon three clear-eyed, deeply-tanned men walked with springy step up the gang-plank of the *Prince George*.

The Dominion Atlantic Railway train *Flying Bluenose* leaving the Yarmouth wharf as the ferry waits in the background.

Photo Album III
He-Woodsmen of the North

A rare licensed guide's pin with No. 1 stamped on the reverse. In his article, Dr. M.B. Miller talked of how the guides earned their "apprenticeship in the lumber camp and on the trail." This photo album expounds upon that, as well as the detailed account of the Nova Scotia Guides' Association covered in *Guides of the North Woods*.

Most rural Nova Scotians during the Elite Sport Tourist Era followed a way of life defined today as seasonal or occupational pluralism, which "represents a strategy for family survival in a marginal world of work … [where] no single activity produces adequate income to meet family needs." Men generally worked the family farm and woodlot for much of the year, with some switching to guide spring and summer fishing parties then hunters in the fall. Winter brought trapping or the annual exodus to lumber camps. At the spring breakup of ice, many worked on the river drives moving logs, then followed up with short-term employment in a sawmill, before planting time signalled the start of a new life cycle back on the farm.

This scene near Ingramport, Halifax County, was typical of timber operations in the mid to late 1800s and early 1900s. Thousands of men and boys left home in late December for a 3- or 4-month exile in lumber camps where they lived a spartan existence, putting in 10- to 12-hour days of back-breaking labour for a dollar a day.

Two young lumberjacks with tools of their trade – axe, crosscut saw and peavey. For an oral history of the Nova Scotia lumber woods, see *Wood Chips & Beans*.

In June 1907, 18 licensed guides from southwestern Nova Scotia met at Yarmouth and formed the Yarmouth County Guides' Association. Shortly thereafter, local chapters sprang up in Annapolis, Digby and Queens counties. During an August 1909 meeting at Milford House, these four county associations were amalgamated into a provincial body, the Nova Scotia Guides' Association, with Eddie Breck elected its first president. According to a newspaper account, "A long toast list, music and dance were followed by play by the guests of the Milford House. The sports were open to the guides of Nova Scotia. A large number of competitors were present from all over the province. The visitors indulged in log rolling [below] and tilting, canoe races [above], canoe carrying and a shooting competition." These four, rare photographs from c.1912 depict similar guide events that Milford House staged to entertain its summer patrons.

Eddie Breck, standing in the bow of the canoe at left, spars with an unidentified guide in a jousting event known as canoe tilting. A victorious Eddie (below) struggles to maintain balance as his vanquished foe takes a dunking.

The Nova Scotia Guides' Association was organized to promote wildlife conservation and to enhance a guide's opportunity to earn a living. While the competitive sports held in conjunction with the annual meeting were intended as a respite from the mundane business side of proceedings, they soon became the marquee attraction, turning the annual get-together into a rendezvous for guides and spectators, similar to the more boisterous and infamous gatherings of mountainmen and fur traders from the century before.

Resembling a decathlon, the formula for a competitor's success at the guides' meet was to enter as many events as humanly possible and place somewhere in the top five of each. Doing so accumulated points, and whoever amassed the most claimed victory. Contestants had to be equally adept on water and dry land, although water sports had the most events including various categories of log rolling and canoe racing. The annual NSGA meet was staged at different locations around Nova Scotia, but its greatest years of success were from 1929 to 1941, when it was held at Lake William, Lunenburg County, as depicted in these two images.

In an event called "canoe humping," a guide stood in the stern and propelled his craft toward the finish line without using poles or paddles by bouncing it up and down through the water.

Gunwale canoe racing involved paddling while standing on the sides or gunwales of a canoe, which may have been an adaptation of the skills and balance required to pole canoes through rapids.

Tub and swimming races were two water events that garnered points in a guide's quest for the grand aggregate championship. The diving tower in these two photos was often the focus of evening entertainment when vaudeville performers thrilled crowds of astonished onlookers with death-defying acts such as jumping from heights of 50 feet into a blazing pool of burning oil or being dropped Harry Houdini-fashion into the lake while confined inside a tied-up burlap bag.

Dry land events included sawing, chopping, shooting, canoe portage and kettle boiling. In this 1950s picture, 2-time overall guide champion Henry Peters (standing at left) watches 5-time grand aggregate winner Watson Peck make the chips fly.

Shooting contests – big rifle, trap, .22 and revolver – drew the largest number of competitors; little wonder when first prize was often a Remington rifle or Winchester trap gun.

Guides also competed in sedate contests such as storytelling, moose calling – performed here by Jim McLeod above on the left – and best tent site as demonstrated below with the father-son team of Owen (left) and Creighton Balcomb, who won the honour on several occasions. The younger Creighton displayed a flair for good-natured showmanship by dressing up in drag in the top right photo to vie for the beauty pageant guide title of Miss Lake William.

Elsie Charles, Laura Whynot Wamboldt, and Flo Whitman. The lady with the rifle is Ivy Bower.

Few women guided or competed in the guides' sports. One who did both, and with great success, was Laura Wamboldt (nee Whynot) from Molega Mines, shown in the left photo, centre, at the 1938 Lake William meet. With Laura are paddling champion Elsie Charles and Flo Whitman, fly casting champion.

Other female competitors of the time included Doris and Viola Peters, sisters of Henry Peters. Women typically competed in same-sex events such as the kettle boil, pancake fry, shooting, and rolling pin toss (for distance, not accuracy). But Laura Wamboldt went head to head against the men, besting them on more than one occasion. She was an expert paddler, log roller and champion pistol shot (note the revolver strapped to her hip), beating all shooters in 1935 and 1936. Laura married Laurie Wamboldt in 1937, one of the top guide competitors, and together they opened Ponhook Lodge near Greenfield, Queens County, which they operated for many years. Their daughters Janet and Elizabeth were both elite log rollers, Elizabeth winning the 1957 women's world title.

Pictured at right is Ivy Bower (68) who guided in Upper Ohio, Shelburne County. She and another lady guide "trimmed all the men" in crosscut sawing at the 1965 meet. *Chatelaine* magazine ran an article on Ivy in its Women of Canada column in July 1966. "Ivy Bower belongs to a vanishing breed: the kind of Nova Scotian who has been called 'hard as nails, soft as butter and independent as pigs on ice.'" Ivy lived up to her hard as nails billing, saying, "I don't like the cities and I don't like the towns and I don't like anybody that does. But up here [Upper Ohio] we got a lot of friends, and there's always the open door."

Many visitors and competitors went to great lengths to establish elaborate campsites for their week-long stay. At the height of the meet's popularity at Lake William, 15,000 to 20,000 people passed through the gates in five days. On one day in 1932, 7,000 spectators, 500 tents and 1,000 cars crowded the grounds, with people arriving from the United States and Scotland. In 1937, CBC Radio provided live coverage from coast to coast. According to one veteran competitor, "If you were a tourist and came to Nova Scotia before the Second World War, the Nova Scotia Guides' Meet was the thing to see."

The New England Sportsmen's Show was staged in 1898 in Boston at the Mechanics Building, shown in the above postcard. A similar spectacle, the New York Sportsmen's Exposition, had been held in 1895 at Madison Square Garden featuring fishing, hunting and related outdoor exhibits.

New Brunswick recognized the tourism potential of the U.S. sportsmen's shows very early, entering a provincial exhibit in 1898 at the Boston Mechanics Building. The Nova Scotia government was slower off the mark, and it was 1930 before records indicate an elaborate display like that pictured here and on page 260 was sent south of the border, a trend that continued in Boston, New York, and Hartford until the outbreak of World War II.

Included among the standard fare of provincial travel literature, maps and motion pictures were live displays of moose, deer, salmon and trout along with native Mi'kmaq demonstrating basketry and guides showcasing traditional woodcraft skills.

When not manning the provincial tourism exhibit, demand was high for members of the Nova Scotia contingent to make guest appearances for a variety of media and entertainment forums. Chief Louis Paul from Lake Albro, above left, demonstrates his moose calling skills for NBC's Lyle Van. Below, a group of guides in lumberjack shirts appear enthralled as part of the stage backdrop for a musical production sung by an "Indian maiden."

As part of an advertising promotional for Ford Charcoal Briquets, 8-time Nova Scotia guide champion Eber Peck from Bear River (above, left) and an unidentified Mi'kmaw guide demonstrate camp cookery skills, then serve up their culinary delight of beans and pancakes to four smiling ladies. The significance of the trophy remains a mystery.

Some of the more than 100 guides who competed at Lake William in the 1930s.

The Nova Scotia Guides' Meets became so popular in the early 1930s that for two years, 1934 and 1935, a 10-day Hunting & Fishing Show and Guides' Tournament was staged in March at the Boston Gardens featuring five teams from the United States and Canada vying for $10,000 in total prize money. On both occasions, Eber Peck won the mantle of North American Champion Guide and Log Roller, along with the more than $500 first place cash award.

Nova Scotia guides dressed in prominent N.S. sweaters pose with competitors from New Brunswick, New Hampshire, Massachusetts, and Maine in 1934 at the Hotel Touraine, Boston. While all participants were paid a $20 bonus just for attending, the Nova Scotia team of 28 was the only one to have its travel expenses paid, lodging provided, and a daily remuneration per man in addition to the standard bonus.

Boston newspapers described the 1934 and 1935 Hunting & Fishing Show and Guides' Tournament at Boston Gardens. On the left is 24-year-old Molly Hunt from Greenfield, Queens County, who with her brother Alan Hunt, a two-time provincial guide champion, attended as part of the Nova Scotia team. In the centre photo is Bill Parker, splitting wood, with his 21-year-old cousin Mal Parker.

Vic Walker from Jordan Falls, Shelburne County, shown here in the kettle boil at Lake William, also competed at Boston. Vic was rumoured to have entertained spectators at the Lake William meets by eating a heavy glass tumbler, followed by several razor blades, a vaudeville stunt he performed – not surprisingly – only once a year.

Mal Parker, above (facing camera), log rolling at the Boston show and below in a promo picture taken in Hollywood, California, c.1950. At right is a program cover from 1934.

Nova Scotia guides Hector MacQuarrie and Watson Peck stand next to the man in a dark suit at the centre of the second row.

Guide Watson Peck kneels far left, front row. Wedged between cowboys in the back row are, left to right, Gerald Buckler, Hector MacQuarrie and Mal Parker. Eber Peck is in the middle row, immediately in front of the cowboy on the right in the back row.

The overwhelming success of the Boston Hunting and Fishing Show and Guides' Tournament made Nova Scotia woodsmen hot commodities for sportsmen's shows that soon opened in Cleveland, Baltimore, Milwaukee, Buffalo, Chicago, Philadelphia, Los Angeles, Detroit, Springfield, Flint, Columbus, Miami, and other cities throughout the United States. The Boston tournament of 1934 and 1935 was based on serious competition, but the sportsmen's shows that followed were intended for entertainment. Small groups of four or five Nova Scotians (like those pictured on the facing page) would take part in the Parade of Outdoor Champions, (shown here in Cleveland), a large travelling production that included a diverse number of acts. Several oral history accounts of performing on the circuit appear in *Guides of the North Woods*.

Illinois Sportsmen's & Vacation Show, Chicago Coliseum, January 16-25, 1948. Left to right: Hector MacQuarrie, Joe King (from Maine), Mal Parker, Eber Peck, Gerald Buckler, Watson Peck. It was not coincidence the Canadians were billed as "He Woodsmen of the North." Pierre Berton writes in *Hollywood's Canada: The Americanization of Our National Image*, "Hollywood preferred to stick to that vast, mythical region, never geographically defined, it invented and called the Northwoods. That was the leading euphemism for Canada in the advertisements. ... It wasn't necessary to mention Canada at all if you talked about the Woods, the Northwoods, the Northwest Woods, or the Great Woods."

Mal Parker (left) and Hector MacQuarrie (centre), both in t-shirts, pose for a photo op at one of the more than 200 exhibits that normally comprised a sportsmen's show.

Bear River's Gerald Buckler sends fellow Bear Riverite Walter Jack for a tumble in the canoe tilt at Gilmore Stadium. The Parade of Outdoor Champions was a professional routine, with full dress rehearsals and time limits for each act. The guides had four minutes to log roll and five minutes for chopping, sawing and canoe tilting. Below is Gilmore Stadium, Los Angeles. Thousands attended the Outdoor Sportsmen's Shows. In the winter of 1951, a touring five-member Nova Scotia team performed their routine before audiences totalling 350,000, in addition to appearing on U.S. television.

Left to right: Eber Peck, Walter Jack, Roy Rogers, Joe King, Gerald Buckler. On occasion "He-Woodsmen of the North" rubbed shoulders with movie stars like Roy Rogers – "The King of the Cowboys" – as well as Clark Gable and Fred McMurray.

Roy Rogers tries his hand at spin casting as his wife Dale Evans looks on. At right, Willard Jack and Gerald Buckler steady the log for Roy as he learns the finer points of log rolling in the tank at Gilmore Stadium.

As the popularity of the Nova Scotia Guides' Meets gradually waned following World War II, a variety of woodsmen's competitions based on its format sprang up throughout the province. The two largest and most popular – both running for 20 years – were the St. Mary's Fish & Game Meet at Stillwater, Guysborough County, (above) and the Shelburne County Sportsmen's Association Meet at Beaver Dam.

Some community events such as the annual Bear River Cherry Carnival, shown here in the 1950s, staged woodsmen's events to entertain the large crowds in attendance. In this photo, hometown hero Eber Peck sends a flailing challenger into the river.

Phil Scott from Barrington, Shelburne County, (left) reached the pinnacle in woodsmen's competitions in 1968 at the age of 20 when he won the world log rolling title, defeating Jubiel Wickheim from British Columbia (above right) at the World Lumberjack Championships in Hayward, Wisconsin. From 1968 to 1980, Phil claimed 4 Canadian, 3 North American, and 9 world championships, 5 in succession. At the time of this writing his nephew Darren Hudson from Barrington was the defending 6-time world champion.

Phil Scott came by his log rolling skills honestly, as at least five generations of the Scott family have worked the lumber woods of Barrington, Shelburne County. Left to right are Phil's grandfather Thomas Scott, great-uncle Uriah Scott, uncle Charles Scott, John Nickerson, Leslie Nickerson, Austin Worthen, Phil's father Tom Scott Jr., and Stan McQuinn.

Stanley Scott, shown above with his Beaver Dam trophy more than half a century ago. Tom Scott Jr. and his four sons — Everett, Stanley, Fred and Phil — dominated the Beaver Dam Meets. All were champions at some point. In fact, for the first 16 years of Beaver Dam one of the five held the championship. While Beaver Dam faded long ago into oblivion, new generations mixed with seasoned family veterans continue to entertain crowds with the Scott Timber Show (see page 278), a professional demonstration of lumberjack skills highlighting 80-year-old Stanley Scott.

Eddie Crouse of South Brookfield, Queens County, holds the paddle he used as a member of the Nova Scotia team in the Centennial Voyageurs Canoe Race, May 24 to September 4, 1967, that covered 3,283 miles from Rocky Mountain House, Alberta, to Expo 67 at Montreal, Quebec. Eddie was a 13-time Nova Scotia guide champion from 1958 to 1983, winning his last title at the age of 64. He also accumulated 190 woodsmen competition awards and participated in 26 sportsmen shows in the United States and Canada.

Conclusion

Much about *The Tent Dwellers* rings true today, lending credence to the adage that the more things change, the more they stay the same. Men still "dig up and tear down and destroy"; whistles are still "set to tooting and bells to jingling"; people still "shriek themselves hoarse" and the world is still an "ugly and discordant" place with "life a short and fevered span in which the soul has a chance to become no more than a feeble and crumpled thing." The main difference from 1908 to 2013 is today's technology provides the means to reach an end in less time and on a grander scale than a century ago, thereby increasing environmental impact and stress levels exponentially. In Albert Bigelow Paine's time he had only the telegraph, telephone and postal service to contend with; all three have been, or are on the verge of being, relegated to the museum of redundancy – thanks to computers, Internet, e-mail, video chat, smart phones, apps, text messaging, Facebook, and Twitter. When Paine wrote about "the preciousness of isolation," he meant escaping to the wilderness, not escaping reality through societal isolation born out of a gaggle of gadgets.

Into the Deep Unknown is unabashedly nostalgic. No apologies are made, but there could be merit in examining reasons for why the book is enamoured with the past. Mark Twain said, "Age is a question of mind over matter. If you don't mind, it doesn't matter." Perhaps that explains it. Having reached the biblical milestone of three score years brings me face to face with the stark reality that there is more time behind than what remains ahead (but hopefully several more than the prophesied additional ten years).

Into the Deep Unknown then could be a mid-life crisis in search of recapturing lost youth. Or perhaps the more than twenty-five years spent researching and writing about the past has entrapped this scribe in a romanticized time warp. That might possibly be, since there's something appealing about yesterday's family values and greater societal sharing and caring, when Sunday was still a day of rest.

A third reason may be found in the maxim that only by looking back and learning from past mistakes can informed decisions be made moving forward into the future. Nowhere does this more aptly apply than the stewardship of our woods and waters. For more than four centuries Nova Scotia's forests have survived the axe, saw, pestilence and fire. The greatest challenge – threat might be a better word – has occurred over the last eighty years with industry laying siege to our natural resources. The devastation has been appalling, widespread and well documented. At the time of this writing, 2012, a sense of troubled calm had descended

Dawn at the edge of the Tobeatic, Sixth Lake, Digby County, 2011. "We are all more or less susceptible to a sort of nostalgia for the woods and waters, where life may be lived in perfect accordance with nature's demands." – Arthur P. Silver, 1907.

upon the land thanks in part to a worldwide catastrophic economic meltdown which has driven Nova Scotia's pulp and paper companies to shutter mills, file for creditor protection and seek government bailouts. The collateral damage is severe economic hardship inflicted upon the thousands who depend on the industry for their livelihood.

Indications are the reprieve from pillaging and plundering may be short-lived, as gluttonous demand for wood fibre to fuel biomass-burning power generators – under the guise of alternative green energy – has become the latest craze proposed by the crazed. Combined with mining interests waiting in the wings for their share of the spoils and a wheezing pulp and paper dinosaur on public life support, spin doctors ratchet up the rhetoric and politicians do what politicians do best, speak in tongues while balancing the tightrope between an increasingly vocal public demand to protect the environment and industry's standard wolf cry of jobs, jobs, jobs.

With large tracts of forest up for grabs and rumours swirling of multi-national companies hovering over the carcass waiting to pounce, the Nova Scotia government purchased half a million acres of defunct pulp-and-paper-owned woodland as part of its commitment to protect twelve percent of Nova Scotia's land mass by 2015. Biodiversity, conservation and sustainable use of natural resources versus rampant, myopic razing of the forests through clear-cutting (and more recently so-called whole-tree harvesting) is a decades-old struggle. With catchphrases like "innovation and change" and "community forestry" emphasized in scripted news releases, many questions arise. Will it be long-term need versus short-term greed? Will common sense prevail over dollars and cents?

Louis and Madeline Harlow, many years after the picture on page 64. All of the original Tent Dwellers are gone today, but their spirits live on at Milford House and in the woods and waters of Kejimkujik and the Tobeatic.

In 2011, these rusting pots and remnants of a cookstove were some of the last artifacts scattered about White Sand Stream and Osborne's Campground.

Only this stone fireplace from the sports' camp stands today on Cossaboom's Point at Sixth Lake, (see page 210), a slowly eroding sentinel from the past.

Milford House is the oldest, continuously run hotel in Nova Scotia, serving travellers for 150 years. Four generations of the Thomas family operated it until 1968 when Ralph Thomas, the last proprietor, passed away. A group of shareholders known as Milford House Properties Ltd. assumed ownership and now manage the historic inn. In 2000, fire totally destroyed the original hotel, but within a year this replica opened for business. For more information, visit www.milfordhouse.ca.

Brochures promoting the 100th anniversary in 2008 of Albert Bigelow Paine's classic. Events included a week-long canoe trip retracing the historic route.

The 2008 Tent Dwellers who paddled the original route to commemorate the 100th anniversary. Left to right, back row: Colin Gray, Dale Dunlop, Bob Thexton, Brian Braganza, Peter McInroy. Front row: Alain Belliveau, Sandra Phinney, Victoria Healy. For more, visit tentdwellers.blogspot.com.

Following are thumbnails of the always popular Scott Timber Show, performing at the Tent Dwellers Festival in Kejimkujik National Park. Events like these keep the tradition of guiding alive.

Crosscut Sawing.

Kettle Boil.

Raymond and Rene Scott, nephews of Phil Scott, log roll wearing roller skates.

Chance, the log burling dog.

Canoe and tub races are part of the show.

Elder statesman of the Scott Timber Show, Stanley Scott, carves a stool with a chain saw.

Brian Braganza and Alain Belliveau paddle a brook between House Lake and Sisketch Lake in the Tobeatic – Mi'kmaq for "Place of the Alder" – during their 2011 quest to find Boundary Rock.

    The Tobeatic, called the Maritime's "last true wilderness," lives on today as though frozen in time. Threatened over the years and soiled but never spoiled, the "Toby," as it is affectionately known, is one of 40 designated wilderness areas in Nova Scotia (as of 2012) protected by the Wilderness Areas Protection Act. One can only hope current and future entrusted stewards show the wisdom of their forefathers and adhere to the "Keep It Wild" motto, preserving the sanctity of the Tobeatic for generations of Tent Dwellers to come.

Portage along west bank of Mersey River from Loon Lake to George Lake.

Tobeatic Dam, between Tobeatic Lake and Little Tupper Lake.

Then away to the heart of the deep unknown,
Where the trout and the wild moose are –
Where the fire burns bright, and the tent gleams white
Under the northern star.
    – Albert Bigelow Paine, *The Tent Dwellers*